THE
CATHOLIC
HIPSTER
HANDBOOK

"*The Catholic Hipster Handbook* is an alt-culture journey into the mysticism, joy, and general weirdness of some new and some too-often-forgotten and unconventional Catholic practices of faith."

From the foreword by **Jeannie Gaffigan**
Writer, producer, director

"The voices in *The Catholic Hipster Handbook* put Catholicism firmly in touch with our present world. The book speaks to the real need for a Church culture that is not only fully Catholic but also culturally authentic. It is also downright hilarious, painfully honest, and appropriately weird at times, too."

Sam Rocha
Editor of the *Patheos* Catholic channel

"Tommy Tighe strikes gold with *The Catholic Hipster Handbook*. Funny, provocative, and serious while not taking themselves too seriously, the contributors will captivate you with their delight in the Lord and their pursuit of the quirky joys hidden in a two-thousand-year history of devotion and prayers in the Catholic Church."

Maria Morera Johnson
Author of *My Badass Book of Saints*

THE CATHOLIC HIPSTER HANDBOOK

Rediscovering Cool Saints, Forgotten Prayers, and Other Weird but Sacred Stuff

TOMMY TIGHE

Founder of CatholicHipster.com

Ave Maria Press AVE Notre Dame, Indiana

To my beautiful wife, Karen, and my incredible
children, James, Paul, Andrew, and Luke.
I haven't slept through the night in years, but I've
loved every moment!

Founded in 1865, Ave Maria Press is a ministry of the United States Province of Holy Cross.

www.avemariapress.com

Paperback: ISBN-13 978-1-59471-707-9

E-book: ISBN-13 978-1-59471-708-6

Cover image of Bishop Karol Wojtyla © CatholicPressPhoto.

Cover and text design by Katherine J. Ross.

Printed and bound in the United States of America.

Library of Congress Cataloging-in-Publication Data

Names: Tighe, Tommy, author.

Title: The Catholic hipster handbook : rediscovering cool saints, forgotten prayers, and other weird but sacred stuff / Tommy Tighe.

Description: Notre Dame : Ave Maria Press, 2017. | Includes bibliographical references and index.

Identifiers: LCCN 2017021026 (print) | LCCN 2017034995 (ebook) | ISBN 9781594717086 (ebook) | ISBN 9781594717079 (pbk. : alk. paper)

Subjects: LCSH: Catholic Church--Miscellanea.

Classification: LCC BX1754 (ebook) | LCC BX1754 .T54 2017 (print) | DDC 282--dc23

LC record available at https://lccn.loc.gov/2017021026

CONTENTS

LIST OF CONTRIBUTORS

FOREWORD

by Jeannie Gaffigan

When my Twitter friend Tommy Tighe reached out to me to write a foreword for his book, I asked the question that any red-blooded American Twitter user would ask: "Does it have to be longer than 140 characters?"

Like many of my cyber friends on Twitter, I have no idea how Tommy and I started following each other. Certainly it was not based on a Twitter suggestion of "Whom to Follow," because I consider those suggestions a personal attack on my character. "Oh yeah, Twitter? You think you know me? Well, just for that, I am purposely *not* going to follow that person. Take *that*."

Maybe it was some brilliant one-liner or something else that caught my attention. But somehow I felt a kindred spirit in Tommy. He was a self-identifying Catholic Guy who was funny and sarcastic and used Homer Simpson–GIFs to describe awkward moments at Mass—an embarrassingly Catholic dude who knew he was embarrassingly Catholic and was not embarrassed by it. Most importantly, my attraction to Tommy's Twitter feed was that he was not preachy or judgy or divisive. His tweets found laughter at his own Catholicness while exposing humor and irony in the sometimes-tragic foibles of our society. It's like, obviously, this bro should write a book.

This collection of essays is an alt-culture journey into the mysticism, joy, and general weirdness of some new and some too-often-forgotten and unconventional Catholic practices of faith. Tommy maps it out for us thematically with the suggestion that these Catholic writers are the ultimate hipsters who are defined by being outside of the cultural mainstream.

These people are the real deal. Reading *The Catholic Hipster Handbook*, I felt like a casual dancer watching a professional production of *Swan Lake*. I often feel that the more I learn about my Catholic faith, the more I realize what a bad Catholic I am. Or maybe that's just the guilt talking. It's awesome to discover that some people out there are transcending the culture by weaving in their love and practice of faithfulness.

Get ready, because you are about to meet some seriously hipster Catholics. You need help deciphering Catholic slang? You're covered. You wanna be down with going "catacombing" to find that perfect unusual baby name? You got it. You need a smartphone app that alerts you throughout the day that it's prayer time (or in my case, an app that alerts me that it's time to feel guilty about something else I'm not doing)? Yeah, baby. It's all up in *The Catholic Hipster Handbook*.

From beard growing to poetry to home-brewing priests, this book of wildly varied writing styles challenges us Catholic-identifying types to look beyond the routines and rituals that define us as "cultural Catholics" who punch the time clock at Mass and check off the sacraments on our to-do lists. In *The Catholic Hipster Handbook*, you're about to go back to the basics for some deep, down-home craft Catholicism.

If you're like, "Whoa! I'm so like *traditional* Catholic. I'm feeling majorly intimidated by all these strange-bearded and bespeckled behaviors!" Well, have no fear, because each essay ends with an "activity" through which you get the opportunity to own your inner hipster based on the suggestions of the authors.

With wit, charm, and talent, Tommy hosts this salon of alt-Catholic writers, storytellers, and poets who express their faith off the beaten path as they navigate through the frenzy of modern society—grabbing onto their spirituality by its organic roots and not letting go.

ACTIVITY

Read the book!

INTRODUCTION

You _____ ho fell in love the first time you went to Mass in th_____ ry Form. Or the gal sneaking a peek at your Brev_____ ng your work meeting. Maybe you're the new _____ sure your kids set up the corn, butter, and cake _____ and her cow on the eve of her relatively unknc____

You _____ re a Catholic hipster, and this is the book you ha____ g for.

For _____ been heading into your local Catholic booksto_____ g to find a book that speaks to you. While the shelves are filled with titles directed at moms, grads, and teens, that special book you'd always hoped would hit you right in your thick-rimmed spectacles and high-top All Stars just hasn't been there.

What you are about to read is a journey into the heart of hipster Catholicism. Yes, it exists, and you have friends out there. The Catholic Church is a 2,000-year-old countercultural community of believers who actually know a thing or two about being hip. But you knew that already.

Packed with stories about cool saints, profound yet forgotten ancient prayers, and the many telltale signs of what it means to be a hipster Catholic, this book is like a hipster CCD, Confirmation, and RCIA program all wrapped into one, sure to help you discover—or rediscover—everything awesome about the Catholic faith. Within these pages, the likes of St. Eligius, St. Isidore the Farmer, Ven. Solanus Casey, and many, many others are waiting for you to discover their inspiring lives of heroic virtue. Ancient and amazing prayers, such as the extended Our Father, the Morning Offering, and the Invocations to the Sacred Heart of Jesus, are waiting to help lead you closer to our Lord and his Blessed Mother. Tales about glasses-wearing, beard-sporting, farmers-market-visiting Catholics not only are going to motivate you to rediscover the faith but will also set you on fire for the Lord!

So, what are you waiting for?

PART ONE

REDISCOVER THE ATTITUDE

There's a certain essence that comes with being Catholic. It's hard to put your finger on it, but it's an attitude unlike that of any other group I have discovered. It's full of paradoxes: of joy amid sadness, hope amid darkness, and other-centered love in a world seemingly dominated by selfishness. It's an attitude that is grounded in being a part of something big, something important—something that is everlasting.

A great many of the things we associate ourselves with in today's world are temporary. Our education, occupations, clubs, groups, products we "can't live without," and even relationships are all missing a certain something, leaving an unmistakable hole that we are desperately trying to fill. We go through life wishing for something deeper, an experience or association more profound.

The Catholic faith is that something we've all been searching for. Two thousand years ago, Jesus Christ himself established a Church, and two thousand years later, he seeks for you to be a part of it. If that isn't cool, I don't know what is.

YOU'RE ROYAL, EVEN IF YOU CAN'T SEE YOUR CROWN

by Sr. Brittany Harrison

It's easy to forget our dignity. Not too many people roll out of bed each morning and dedicate the first moments of their days to straightening their spiritual crowns and greeting their king, but the saints teach us that we should do exactly that. St. Josemaría Escrivá calls the first minute of the day the "heroic minute" and encourages everyone to get up at the first sound of the alarm and devote those first moments to prayer, sanctifying the day. If you're anything like me, this is easier said than done.

The First Letter of Peter tells us that "you are 'a chosen race, a royal priesthood, a holy nation, a people of his own, so that you may announce the praises' of him who called you out of darkness into his wonderful light" (1 Pt 2:9). God not only created us and brought us into existence but God also chose us, made us his own special possession, and gave us dignity—regal dignity. This royal priesthood allows us to add our voices to the hymn of praise to God's mercy arising from every corner of creation and to intercede for one another in prayer.

Our spiritual enemy, the Accuser, the devil, wants us to forget our dignity by tossing away our royal crown through sin

3

and fear. He is clever in his attacks, suggesting that our happiness lies in acts we know to be wrong and then accusing us of having no value after we commit the sin. He feigns friendship and concern for our happiness one moment, and like the snake in the garden of Eden, he rejects us as worthless the next. To add to the pain, he tries to persuade us through shame that God could not possibly forgive such evil, and he makes every effort to keep us from the sacrament of Reconciliation.

The best ways to keep our spiritual crowns sparkling and in place are through the sacraments and daily prayer. Through daily prayer, even from the first moment of the day, we can remind ourselves that we are called to live as royal children of God, and we can gain the daily strength we need for whatever, and whomever, we encounter. For many saints, going to daily Mass to receive the Eucharist was a necessity, but if our vocations and/or jobs do not allow us such a gift, we can make Spiritual Communions and ask Jesus to come into our hearts through our desire to receive the Eucharist. Monthly Confession, praying of the Rosary, reading scripture, and having good friends who share our values are also aids in keeping our crowns in place and enriching them with beauty. In moments of difficulty, times of temptation, and struggles with discouragement, the discipline of a strong prayer life will anchor us in the love of God and keep our crowns where they are meant to be—adorning the heads of children beloved by God, not because we can or did earn his love but because of the freely given, incredible love shown to us in Christ Jesus, our Lord. "But God proves his love for us in that while we were still sinners Christ died for us" (Rom 5:8).

COOL SAINT:
BL. AUGUSTUS CZARTORYSKI

When Bl. Augustus Czartoryski was born in 1858, his family, the royal family of Poland, was in exile in Paris. His parents raised the young Augustus to be aware of his regal dignity, but God had other plans for him.

As his family planned a suitable match for him, Augustus discerned God's will for his life, often speaking of how he tired of royal banquets and ceremonies. He felt that God called him to do something *more* with his life, something radical. When he was twenty-five, Augustus met St. John Bosco, the founder of the Salesians, at the Mass he offered in the Lambert Castle chapel in Paris. Following that encounter, Augustus went to Turin to visit Don Bosco as often as his father would allow him. Again and again he asked Don Bosco to allow him to join the Salesians, but Don Bosco refused him, citing his royal crown and life of luxury as being big hurdles to overcome in order to join the literally poor and demanding life of the Salesians.

Not one to take a no lightly, Augustus asked Pope Leo XIII to intercede for him, and the pope sent word to Don Bosco through Augustus to "tell Don Bosco that it is the Pope's will that he receives you among the Salesians."[1] Don Bosco relented.

Prince Augustus soon became Fr. Augustus and did not permit anyone to speak of his royal lineage, nor did he refer to it himself. The only crown he desired was the one given to him in Baptism and which he daily strove to beautify through holiness.

Along with royal lineage, he also inherited poor health from his family. After several years of priesthood, Fr. Augustus died of tuberculosis, nursed by his close friend from the novitiate, Ven. Andrew Beltrami. After Fr. Augustus's death, a hundred men from Poland asked to join the Salesians, inspired by the example of their prince. Eventually, the Salesians sent missionaries to Poland who opened an underground seminary in which St. John Paul II would study during World War II. Thus the royal and holy influence of Bl. Augustus Czartoryski impacted not only those closest to him but also the world.

Bl. Augustus Czartoryski, pray for us.

FORGOTTEN PRAYER

This prayer from Psalms is the motto that Bl. Augustus chose:

> How lovely your dwelling, O Lord of hosts! My soul yearns and pines for the courts of the Lord. . . . Better one day in your courts than a thousand elsewhere. (Ps 84:2–3a, 11)

ACTIVITY

Complete the crown below by embellishing it in any way you like. This crown is a symbol of the spiritual dignity you bear as a child of God. Add any images, decorations, words, or colors you would like to represent your relationship with God.

WE DO THINGS THE HARD WAY

by Steven Lewis

There's no point in fighting it: St. Francis of Assisi is the patron saint of Catholic hipsters. Name any obscure, hip, and cool saint you want; it all comes down to Frank. If you pay attention to his life, you will quickly find out that he did everything the hard way. From his pursuit of poverty to his desire for perfection to frickin' *asking for the stigmata*, there was no easy faith for this guy.

This is a trait that he has left behind to his true spiritual sons and daughters, the Catholic hipsters. We draw this both from our ever-long quest for authenticity and from our Catholicism—with its stone altars and meatless Fridays. Throughout our lives we have known people who have left the Church and lost their faith because quick answers repeated over time just aren't able to do justice to some of the tragedies of life. Easy excuses for Christianity just don't cut it. We know a life well lived and a faith well practiced are going to be hard, so we need our prayers, art, living, and entertainment to be tough enough to help us survive.

As Catholic hipsters, we know that cheap faith is what makes people stop trusting in God. Chances are, you've built

a distaste for at least one of these things. You're not required
to dislike them; it's just more likely that you might reject these:

- hand signals
  Yes, Lord, yes, Lord, yes yes, Lord, I will never do that
  again.
- cheesy church songs
  It's a mark of spiritual maturity to outgrow "Lord, I Lift
  Your Name on High," "You Are Mine," and "City of God."
  It's okay; you can let them go.
- newfangled spiritual books
  Yeah, your *Napoleon Dynamite* devotional is cute, but have
  you ever picked up *Divine Intimacy*?
- short novels
  Why are you reading *The Alchemist* when *The Brothers Kara-
  mazov* and *Kristin Lavransdatter* lie unread on your shelf?
- any American writer who isn't Flannery O'Connor
  Now you're just wasting my time. Break out her novels and
  short stories, and brace yourself for the greatness.

This is why you'll find Catholic hipsters learning the Angelus and reciting it three times a day, humming old hymns,
taking spiritual cues from the Carthusians (the most intense
Catholic monks in the world), and only watching religious
movies that get *really* sad before they get close to being happy.

This is not a life of cheap, easy prayers full of cheap, easy
answers. Try it the hard way; you'll see the difference.

COOL SAINT: ST. EPAPHRAS

It's amazing how Epaphras, the bishop of Colossae, St. Paul's
prison buddy, and a man name-dropped by Paul *three times*
in two different letters of the New Testament (see Colossians
1:6–8, Colossians 4:12, and Philemon 1:23), could go totally
unnoticed. Colossians describes Epaphras as "striving" or

"struggling" for Christians in his prayer, and that's why I like him. In many languages, including Spanish and Greek, the word for *strive* or *struggle* is the same word for *wrestle* or *fight*. It's similar to how the Spanish word *luchar* can mean a political struggle, while a *luchador* is a professional wrestler. Think of Epaphras as a heavenly masked wrestler, pile-driving Satan for you in prayer when you don't have the strength.

FORGOTTEN PRAYER

The *Te Deum* is the perfect prayer for people who like to do things the hard way, because it's so long:

> You are God: we praise you;
> You are the Lord: we acclaim you;
> You are the eternal Father:
> All creation worships you.
> To you all angels, all the powers of heaven,
> Cherubim and Seraphim, sing in endless praise:
> Holy, holy, holy, Lord, God of power and might,
> heaven and earth are full of your glory.
> The glorious company of apostles praise you.
> The noble fellowship of prophets praise you.
> The white-robed army of martyrs praise you.
> Throughout the world the holy Church acclaims you:
> Father, of majesty unbounded,
> your true and only Son, worthy of all worship,
> and the Holy Spirit, advocate and guide.
> You, Christ, are the king of glory,
> the eternal Son of the Father.
> When you became man to set us free
> You did not shun the Virgin's womb.
> You overcame the sting of death,
> and opened the kingdom of heaven to all believers.
> You are seated at God's right hand in glory.

We believe that you will come and be our judge.
Come then, Lord, and help your people,
bought with the price of your own blood,
and bring us with your saints
to glory everlasting.
Save your people, Lord, and bless your inheritance.
Govern and uphold them now and always.
Day by day we bless you.
We praise your name for ever.
Keep us today, Lord, from all sin.
Have mercy on us, Lord, have mercy.
Lord, show us your love and mercy;
For we put our trust in you.
In you, Lord, is our hope:
And we shall never hope in vain.

ACTIVITY

We all know some famous pilgrimages around the world: walking the Camino de Santiago; traveling to Jerusalem, Fatima, Rome, and Guadalupe; and even attending World Youth Day is a pilgrimage. But there are a variety of pilgrimage sites much closer to home; just look for anything called a shrine. A shrine is, by definition, a destination for pilgrimage. It can be an entire church or just a side chapel in a larger church, but it is there as a place for you to travel to so you can pray. Shrines are always dedicated to specific saints or devotions, and they are closer than you think.

Go to Google right now and type "shrine near me." Suddenly, you have a local pilgrimage you can get to! This is the important part: don't get there the easy way. Don't just drive there. If you can, walk. If you must, use public transportation. Pack a backpack with prayers, a lunch, and extra cash or food you can give to people who ask for it. Get lost. Ask for help from a stranger. Risk the elements. Risk getting mugged.

Risk the discomfort. Then when you finally get to your local shrine and start praying, you'll realize the truth about pilgrimages: you were praying the whole time.

CATHOLIC SLANG

by Sergio Bermudez

So that attractive person at Mass has finally invited you to the hidden grotto where all the hip Catholics congregate, and you're feeling great. You show up, looking fresh, prepared to make some friends and be brought into the fold. All of a sudden, you think to yourself, "What are these people saying? I understand some of the words; it's clearly English, but it's not making sense."

Terms and phrases such as *emotional chastity, intentionality,* and *guard your heart* are all rather confusing to the uninitiated. So, I've gathered some of these terms and phrases (and also made up a few that I hope will catch on) to help you navigate a strange, perhaps new, avenue, so you won't be left behind in the conversation:

- *Catholic thirst*—That dude/girl who wants to get married but doesn't really care who that future spouse is. Their reasons for marriage are suspect, and they tend to evaluate everyone's potential for marriage. Often found at Catholic gatherings trying not to salivate at members of the opposite gender.
- *Emotional chastity*—This is perhaps the weirdest term, and it's not always clearly defined—even though everyone writes about it.

It's basically asking you to be disciplined with your emotions. Much like *guard your heart* (see below), just play it cool.

- *Guard your heart*—This isn't some veiled threat. It's another dating thing. This one's saying: Don't get too anxious or start planning that wedding right away. Just be cool. Always.
- *How is your heart?*—This isn't a question about your health. It is more a way to ask how you are feeling on a deep, emotional level.
- *Intentionality*—Used in dating. Again. Basically, people want to know your goals with a relationship. This is tricky when starting out because you don't want to be that thirsty person but you also don't want to be jumping into a relationship for the wrong reasons. Choose your answer wisely if asked about this.
- *Nunnabe*—Wannabe nun. She'll talk a lot about how she can't wait to go to the convent.
- *Predestinationships*—The idea of soul mates or that your relationship was somehow preordained—cause y'know, free will is a thing.
- *Steubies*—Kids who went to Franciscan University of Steubenville. You'll recognize them because they'll literally know every other Catholic in the area. They almost all know each other; I don't know how such a thing is possible, but that's how it goes.
- *Tradbro*—A devout Catholic who is also a bro. As the name suggests, the Tradbro falls more on the conservative/traditional end of the Catholic spectrum. He is aware of his bro-ness, which is why we all like him and tolerate him.
- *STREAM*—St. Thomas Rules Everything Around Me. Handy for when you are kicking it with a crew of Thomists.

There are more, of course, and as with most matters of language, they are flexible, so take some time to familiarize yourself with the informal lexicon we Catholics employ. Hopefully this helps the next time you're at a kickback with a handful of Catholic pals. Be sure to drop any of these terms and watch everyone stand impressed at the smooth way you have with

Catholic communication. When you do, it will become clear to all around that you are a certified Catholic hipster.

COOL SAINT:
ST. FRANCIS DE SALES

The author of one of the most influential spiritual books of all time, St. Francis de Sales has somehow managed to remain an obscure saint among most pew-sitting Catholics. St. Francis is the patron of authors and writers and knew a thing or two about the power of language and the impact of the words we choose.

He was quite fond of using flyers and books to convert Calvinists (what most Protestants were called in his time and place), and by all accounts he was good at it. His *Introduction to the Devout Life* continues to be one of the most important books on Catholic spirituality and an incredible guide through our journey toward holiness despite being written more than four hundred years ago.

St. Francis de Sales once said, "Do not wish to be anything but what you are, and try to be that perfectly." Through his intercession, may we achieve baby steps toward that goal each and every day.

St. Francis de Sales, pray for us.

FORGOTTEN PRAYER

> My God, I give you this day. I offer you, now, all of the good that I shall do, and I promise to accept, for love of you, all of the difficulty that I shall meet. Help me to conduct myself during this day in a manner pleasing to you. Amen.
>
> —St. Francis de Sales

ACTIVITY

If we want to be on a path to hipster holiness, we've got to be on the cutting edge of Catholic cool. And to be on the cutting edge, we need to come up with our own Catholic slang. Come up with some new phrases to toss around, and try them out at the donut table after Mass next Sunday.

If people look at you with a weird look, you've probably come up with a good one!

HOW GLASSES DO MORE
THAN HELP US TO SEE

by Sarah Vabulas

When you wear glasses, you just *feel* smarter. I'm not sure what it is, but you pop them on your face and voila! You feel like a genius.

When asked to think about glasses and what they mean to us as Catholics and as hipsters, my immediate thought was of librarians and ridiculously smart theologians who pour over books written by greats such as St. Thomas Aquinas, St. Augustine, and St. Teresa of Avila and those by modern-day theologians known for brilliant writing and insight, such as Benedict XVI. It's what I've secretly aspired to be since I began to study and unpack some of these books in my college theology classes. To me, these theologians are the ultimate hipsters—that is, until we add St. John Paul II into the mix.

There are several photos that regularly make rounds on social media showing then–Bishop Karol Wojtyla rocking glasses that were regular for his time but have boomeranged to become hipster in ours. I own two pairs myself, but the truth is, I just like how they look on me and how they make me feel more confident. Isn't that the point of anything we wear, anyway?

When I was growing up, anyone who wore glasses was called "four eyes" or a nerd. Watch any movie about kids, and you'll notice it's a common insult. But now, wearing glasses is cool, a fact that never fails to me amaze me.

I always wanted glasses as a kid. I didn't care that people made fun of them. I thought they were such a great way to express yourself in a unique way. It's easy to show up at school wearing the same shoes or clothes, but glasses become the essence of you. They're often one of the first things anyone sees when looking at you. When I was in college, it became a challenge to read the chalkboard or the overhead when I didn't sit in one of the front rows. I had my eyes tested, and it turned out I had less-than-perfect distance vision and needed corrective lenses. Finally! My day had come, and I could feel cool.

Sunglasses also make a person feel cool. I remember when I was allowed my first pair of nice sunglasses and got a pair of Ray-Bans. I went to Savannah, Georgia, on a trip with my Girl Scouts troop, and during a trip to the restroom, those specs ended up in the Savannah sewer system. I was in tears. But I learned an important life lesson that day: take care of the nice things you receive, or they might be flushed down the toilet.

As a Catholic, that is a lesson we can embrace in all that we do. The blessing God bestows upon us should not be dismissed or easily thrown away. We ought to praise and thank him for his generosity and for his great love of each of us as individuals, as persons with our own styles and our own brand of cool—glasses or not.

The need for glasses calls to mind the stories in the synoptic gospels of the blind man asking Jesus to heal him:

> Now as he approached Jericho a blind man was sitting by the roadside begging, and hearing a crowd going by, he inquired what was happening. They told him, "Jesus of Nazareth is passing by." He shouted,

"Jesus, Son of David, have pity on me!" The people
walking in front rebuked him, telling him to be silent,
but he kept calling out all the more, "Son of David,
have pity on me!" Then Jesus stopped and ordered that
he be brought to him; and when he came near, Jesus
asked him, "What do you want me to do for you?"
He replied, "Lord, please let me see." Jesus told him,
"Have sight; your faith has saved you." He immediately received his sight and followed him, giving glory
to God. When they saw this, all the people gave praise
to God. (Lk 18:35–43)

If only I approached the Lord with such passion each day,
begging Jesus to have pity on me and save me from my sins
and ailments! So while I'm pretty sure my eyesight won't be
healed anytime soon, I'll embrace the gift of wearing glasses
that represent my style and rock them for the Lord, knowing
he's with me all the while.

COOL SAINT: ST. JEROME

I first learned of St. Jerome when I began to study the Bible
more deeply in high school, learning that he is best known
for translating the Bible from Greek and Hebrew into Latin,
making the book more accessible to people of his time. While
glasses didn't exist when St. Jerome was alive, he is often
depicted with glasses in many of his images. His feast day is
September 30, when we celebrate him as the patron saint of
spectacle makers.

FORGOTTEN PRAYER

A Prayer for Christ's Mercy

O Lord, show your mercy to me and gladden my
heart. I am like the man on the way to Jericho who

was overtaken by robbers, wounded, and left for dead. O Good Samaritan, come to my aid. I am like the sheep that went astray. O Good Shepherd, seek me out and bring me home in accord with your will. Let me dwell in your house all the days of my life and praise you for ever and ever with those who are there. Amen.

—St. Jerome

ACTIVITY

Donate a pair of glasses!

Many of us are blessed to have the access and means to purchase glasses and other corrective eyewear. It is our duty as Catholics to give back to those who do not. Consider purchasing from Warby Parker or another company that gives a pair when you buy a pair.[2] Find ways to donate in your community for those in need so they too can see the beautiful world in front of them as we do.

THE CUTTING EDGE OF FASHION

by Sr. Brittany Harrison

What we wear gives people clues about who we are. As a religious sister who wears a habit (the distinctive clothing of a male or female religious), people look at me and instantly understand certain things about me. If the persons looking have seen movies such as *The Sound of Music* or *Sister Act*, they probably realize that I am Catholic and a nun. Those who have never encountered nuns or religious sisters in real life or cinema might be confused. Regardless of whether or not they comprehend what my clothing means, most people immediately understand that it means *something*.

Before I became a Salesian, I prided myself on always being well dressed. I liked to dress in bright colors and loved anything exotic looking. My aesthetic was boho chic, and I was usually ahead of the fashion trends and over them by the time everyone else started buying them in mainstream stores. I was not, by any stretch of the imagination, what anyone would consider a "fashionista," but I always looked nice. I wanted people to know, when they looked at me, that I had dignity and good taste.

Why should anyone care about what we wear? Because our clothes speak. How I dress can tell people certain things about me, such as what colors I like, what sports teams I support, and what culture I identify with. In the Theology of the Body teachings of St. John Paul II, we learn that the human body reveals God, and our clothing can either increase the depth of that revelation or conceal it; this is called the *sacramentality of the body*. Our bodies are visible signs of God's invisible love. How I present myself to others sends a message about how I view myself as a child of God. Sloppy clothing can communicate a poor self-image or a person who is overwhelmed, whereas even the simplest attire, well arranged, can reveal God's beauty to the world through us.

Next time you get dressed, take a long look in the mirror. What are your clothes communicating to others? Are they sending a message you don't intend, or are they revealing, more fully, who you are in the best sense? You don't have to wear a nun's habit to show other people God's presence through your life, but wearing clothing that doesn't distract from your dignity and true value can certainly help. Be fashionable, be cutting edge, but most of all, be the real you!

St. Francis de Sales, the saint after whom the Salesians get our name, once declared, "Be who you are and be that well!" Pretty good advice, even when it comes to fashion!

COOL SAINT: ST. MARIA DOMENICA MAZZARELLO

St. Maria Domenica Mazzarello loved fashion as a young woman; in fact, she was known for always having the best clothes. Her family did not have a lot of money, but she learned how to embroider and decorate even the simplest dresses in order to make them stand out. She was the fashion icon of her Italian village. Her hair was always perfect, her shoes were always shined, and her clothes were always tastefully arranged. Fashion was how Maria expressed herself, but fashion also distracted her from her most real self.

The pastor of her parish, Fr. Dominic Pestarino, once told Maria to put some grease on her boots so they would not be so shiny and attract so much attention. This suggestion caused Maria to do some deep soul-searching about why she was focusing so much on her external appearance while somewhat neglecting the beauty of her soul. Maria learned how to be a seamstress and taught girls how to create their own clothing, using her experience with fashion to bring them joy and confidence.

Later in life, Maria helped found the Salesian Sisters with St. John Bosco. The educational mission of the Salesian Sisters continues today, all over the world, inspired by the witness of St. Maria Mazzarello, who reminds us that "a joyful heart is the sign of a heart that loves the Lord very much."

St. Maria Domenica Mazzarello, pray for us.

FORGOTTEN PRAYER

Dear Mother Mary, ever Virgin, help me to save my soul.

–St. John Bosco

ACTIVITY

Match the Catholic clothing item to its proper name and definition. Start by writing each word and each definition on separate pieces of paper. Mix them up. Get a group of Catholic hipster friends, and see who can match the words with the definition the quickest.

> *Alb*—A symbol of innocence and purity, the alb is a long robe worn by the priest underneath the stole and chasuble during the Mass. It is tied at the waist with a cincture.

Amice—An oblong piece of white cloth wrapped around a priest's neck, partially under the alb. It symbolizes the helmet of salvation. It is optional if the alb covers a priest's ordinary clothing.

Biretta—A square, stiff, tufted hat that may be worn by clergy.

Cappa—A long cape worn during liturgical services by Carmelites and Dominicans.

Cassock—A full-length buttoned robe worn by clergy, available in various styles and cuts. Often, it has thirty-three buttons to symbolize the thirty-three years of the life of Christ. The basic color is black, but additional colors added to the black are significant. The pope's cassock is white.

Chasuble—A symbol of charity and unselfish service for the Lord, this is the outer garment worn by a priest and is often bell-shaped. Its color typically reflects the color of the liturgical season.

Cincture—The cord that is worn over the alb by the priest, which symbolizes chastity.

Dalmatic—A sleeved tunic worn by a deacon and matching the liturgical color. It's a symbol of joy and happiness in God's service.

Devotional scapular—Two small, typically postage-sized pieces of fabric that are attached by string and worn over the chest and back by those who are devoted to our Lady. It's considered a miniature version of the monastic one of the Carmelites.

Fisherman's ring—The ring worn by the pope, containing his personal seal. It is destroyed after the pope dies.

Habit—The particular outfit worn by members of a religious congregation. The color and cut distinguish the different congregations, much like athletic uniforms differentiate teams.

Humeral veil—A long, rectangular piece of fabric that is worn across the shoulders by clergy during processions and Benediction with the Blessed Sacrament. It has long ends that hang down the front and cover the hands of the cleric but may also be used to cover the ciborium containing the Blessed Sacrament.

Maniple—Ornamental vestment worn by the priest over the left forearm. It looks like a small arm stole. It symbolizes the hard work and suffering a priest must expect in his vocation.

Mitre—The tall, pointed hat worn by a bishop.

Monastic scapular—A piece of ankle-length fabric that hangs down the front and back of a monastic outfit and is symbolic of service.

Pallium—A thin, white wool band of fabric, with front and back extensions and decorated with black crosses, that is symbolic of apostolic authority. It's only worn by the pope, archbishops, and patriarchs.

Sister's veil / Nun's veil—A piece of cloth that covers the head of a female religious and is symbolic of her consecration to God.

Stole—A long, colored piece of fabric that is worn like a long scarf over the shoulders of a priest and hangs down the front. It symbolizes priestly authority and is worn whenever a priest is engaged in a sacrament.

Surplice—A knee-length white vestment worn by seminarians and priests over a cassock.

Zucchetto—A circular black (for priests), magenta (for bishops), red (for cardinals), or white (for the pope) skullcap worn by clergy.

TAKING POPE FRANCIS TO THE FARMERS MARKET

by Mary Rezac

If it's a Saturday in the summertime, there's a good chance you'll find me and some of my fellow Catholic hipsters perusing the peaches and baby kale at a local farmers market.

When I lived in Nebraska, it was the cobbled streets of the Haymarket in Lincoln where I would leisurely spend my sunny Saturdays picking out produce and sipping hipster coffee. I knew which booths had the best breakfast burritos, the prettiest flowers, and the heartiest, most obscure-looking desk-sized cacti and succulents. I could quickly scope out the best-priced summer produce and the most authentic kolaches.

Moving to Denver, Colorado, I had to start again from scratch, but it wasn't a tiresome chore. Nothing says cool, hipster friend date like, "Hey, let's check out the farmers market on Pearl Street!"

There was always something about buying local, farm-to-table fare at a farmers market that spoke to my raised-on-a-Nebraska-farm soul. I grew up knowing that tomatoes from the garden are redder and richer than those from the store and that if you aren't eating farm-fresh eggs, you probably shouldn't be eating eggs at all.

Still, it wasn't until recently that I began realizing why the concept of farmers markets also spoke to my Catholic hipster soul.

The first time the appeal of the farmers market hit me, I was doing something any good hipster Catholic should—drinking craft beer at a Theology on Tap event in Denver. Two priests (one bearded, one not, for those wondering) from the podcast *Catholic Stuff You Should Know* were speaking about consumerism and Catholicism, two things I never thought had much to do with each other. But it's the Catholic Church we're talking about here, and at the end of the day, you'd be hard-pressed to find a subject that she, being the good mother she is, hasn't addressed.

Over the hour they had, the priests explained how the Catholic teaching of subsidiarity applies to the buying process: we should try, as best we are able, to get goods and services from their most direct sources, because this puts the human person back in the center of the exchange. In a culture that's become unhealthily detached from material goods, how they are made, and their true value, buying local at places like a farmers market is one step we can all take to reorder the way we think about the goods we consume and the people behind them.

I'd never before heard how one could be *unhealthily* detached from material goods, so here's an example: I once worked at a summer camp, and we were having a cookout. My cabin of ten-year-old girls had just seated themselves at a creaky picnic table and, when they weren't chowing down on their hot dogs and hamburgers, started talking about how they wanted to be vegetarians, because they didn't want to harm animals. I smiled at the irony of the situation and said, "But you're eating hot dogs, and those are made out of meat."

"No they're not!" one of the girls retorted.

"Oh really?" I asked. "Then where do they come from?"

"They come from the store!" the girls responded.

Yes, even in Nebraska, one of the top states for beef production, these girls were so detached from the production and
origin of their food that they had no concept of how the fare
they were eating came to be.

But that's the beauty of the farmers market. At the flower
booth, I can compliment the woman and her two daughters on
their beautiful zinnias, and that might lead to a conversation
about their favorite flowers or how it's been a really good year
for zinnias compared to last summer. I can tell the kolach man
that his pastries remind me of my grandma Rezac's, and he can
tell me that potato flakes are his secret ingredient.

At the very least, a farmers market makes me look the seller
in the eye and smile, and I know that the item I'm purchasing
personally cost that person time and effort to create or produce.
This lets me build some sort of relationship and sense of community with the people directly involved in the production of
the goods I'm buying and puts the human person back in the
center of the buying process, which "ought to be the principle,
the subject and the end of all social institutions" (*CCC*, 1881).

COOL SAINT:
ST. ISIDORE THE FARMER

While he's not exactly obscure in the Catholic farm fields of
Nebraska, I'm not sure how much attention St. Isidore is receiving in other parts of the Catholic world, hipster and not, and
he's deserving of some major hipster cred.

A farmer from Spain, St. Isidore entered the service of a
wealthy landowner from Madrid at a young age; he would
work there for the rest of his life. He married a simple woman
and brought her home to heaven with him; she's also a canonized saint—St. Maria de la Cabeza (#marriagegoals, amiright?).
They had one son, who died as a child.

St. Isidore was known for being deeply religious; he spent his days behind the plow in prayer and even annoyed his fellow workers for spending too much time in church. He had a love for animals and for people, particularly the poor. Some accounts of his life say that he received visions from heaven, that angels helped him in his work, and that he miraculously provided the poor with food on several occasions.

He's a rare breed of saint—married, not very learned, and a man in touch with the Lord and the land.

FORGOTTEN PRAYER

Prayer of the Christian Farmer

O God, Source and Giver of all things,
Who manifests your infinite majesty,
power, and goodness in the earth about us,
we give you honor and glory.
For the sun and rain,
for the manifold fruits of our fields,
for the increase of our herds and flocks we thank you.
For the enrichment of our souls with divine grace, we
    are grateful.
Supreme Lord of the harvest,
graciously accept us and the fruits of our toil,
in union with Christ your Son,
as atonement for our sins,
for the growth of your Church,
for peace and charity in our homes,
for salvation to all. Amen.[3]

ACTIVITY

The Catholic hipster farmers market scorecard!

It's a summer Saturday morning, and you're dressed in your Catholic hipster best, which may or may not include hipster sandals, your grandma's sweater, and some jeans you thrifted last week.

Now hop on your hybrid bicycle and get over to the nearest farmers market you can find. Once you're there, pull out this scorecard and see how you and your friends do. The loser buys everyone something organic.

- Make it to daily Mass beforehand: 20 points
- Convince friends at said Mass to join you for farmers market fun: 10 points
- Use a bicycle, walk, or take public transportation to arrive at the farmers market: 5 points
- Casually evangelize to friends already at the farmers market when you tell them about said Mass: 10 points
- Purchase coffee from a local, non-chain coffee shop to drink while browsing: 5 points
- Casually evangelize to someone when they ask about your scapular/miraculous medal/rope rosary bracelet/other religious apparel: 10 points
- Spot someone else wearing scapular/miraculous medal/rope rosary bracelet/other religious apparel and give them a knowing smile: 10 points
- Buy something Catholic from someone who is Catholic: 15 points
- Casually slip "subsidiarity" into farmers market conversation: 20 points
- Find a vegetable or pastry that convincingly resembles Jesus or Mary: 20 points
- Meet someone you've seen at your parish but haven't talked to: 20 points
- Buy something with the words "organic," "local," or "gluten free" in the name: 5 points per label

TOTAL: _____ points

CATHOLIC WEIRD ON TWITTER

by Tommy Tighe

Ah, Twitter. Depending on where you sit at any given moment, the Twitterverse is either one of the greatest things on earth or one of the worst. It can be both a tool that brings us together and a wedge that splits us apart.

In case you don't know, the larger Twitterverse is made up of many smaller Twitter Galaxies (I made that up), little pockets of Twitter that only appeal to those within a certain group.

All you have to do is click on that tiny little bird, and you're instantly thrown headfirst into a wide variety of topics. There's everything from Political Twitter (more than you would ever want to know about candidates and politics) to Blizzard Twitter (when there's a big storm brewing) to Beer Drinking Twitter (keeping up with all your favorite breweries and beer drinkers) to Trashy TV Twitter (#Bachelor is alive and strong, believe it or not)—and, not to be outdone, there's Catholic Twitter.

Catholic Twitter is a weird and wonderful place, much like *Cheers*, where everybody knows your name, and while it may sound a tad overwhelming, let me assure you, Catholic Twitter is one of the greatest places on the Internet. Here's why:

Have you ever wanted to say something about your pro-life views as loudly and proudly as you can but feared the nasty backlash that comes from standing up on your desk while shouting "Defund Planned Parenthood!" at your coworkers?

Catholic Twitter is there for you.

Have you ever wanted to make a joke about the difference between transubstantiation and consubstantiation using a GIF from the Tom Hanks movie *Big* but were afraid nobody would get the joke?

Catholic Twitter is there for you.

And it's not all silliness.

Have you ever wanted to see unbiased coverage of various underreported events such as the March for Life and the many papal visits around the world?

Catholic Twitter is there for you.

Have you ever wanted to mobilize thousands to pray for an intention that has been weighing heavily on your heart?

Catholic Twitter is really there for you.

Sure, it's just a silly little app, one that we waste a lot of time on, but it's also a very clear and modern explanation of how the Body of Christ is working and moving in today's world. It's an opportunity to see the Body of Christ standing up for you and the Church founded by Christ.

It's also really nice to know you're not alone.

COOL SAINT:
BL. JAMES ALBERIONE

James Alberione was an Italian priest and founder of the Society of St. Paul, the Daughters of St. Paul, and many other religious institutes that make up what has come to be known as the Pauline family.

Bl. James understood very well the need to evangelize the culture through the means of modern technology and the media, and he made it his mission to ensure that Catholic evangelization would be on the forefront of new ways to get the message out there.

If he were alive today, he would most definitely have a Twitter account, as evidenced by the fact that his Daughters of St. Paul are some of the most widely known Catholic tweeters out there.

Bl. James passed on to his eternal reward on November 26, 1971, just an hour after meeting with Pope Paul VI in Rome. He was beatified by Pope John Paul II in 2003.

Bl. James Alberione, pray for us.

FORGOTTEN PRAYER

Prayer through the intercession of Bl. James Alberione

Lord, glorify Bl. James Alberione
    in your Church.
Let him be for all of us a light.
Guide and support the work of
    our sanctification and in our apostolate.
Open the way for evangelization
so that the presence of Jesus Master,
the Way, the Truth, and the Life,
may shine on the world through Mary,
Mother and Queen of the Apostles.
Grant me the grace I am praying for . . . (*mention your*
    petition)
(*Say an* Our Father, Hail Mary, *and* Glory Be)
Jesus Master, the Way, the Truth, and the Life, have
    mercy on us.
Mary, Queen of the Apostles, pray for us.
St. Paul the Apostle, pray for us.
From all sin, deliver us, O Lord.
      —Prayer given to me by the Daughters of St. Paul

ACTIVITY

Have you heard about how cool Catholic Twitter is but no clue where to start? No problem!

Here's how you start: download the Twitter app on your smartphone, and start following all the totally awesome Catholics who are sharing the faith and cracking jokes all at the same time!

Here's a handy list of my top folks to follow: Jennifer Fulwiler (@JenFulwiler), Jim Gaffigan (@JimGaffigan), Jeannie Gaffigan (@JeannieGaffigan), Matt Swaim (@MattSwaim), Danielle Bean (@DanielleBean), Eye of the Tiber (@EyeOfTheTiber), Leah Darrow (@LeahDarrow), Angry Catholic (@AngryCatholic), Sergio Bermudez (@NostromoSerg), Haley Stewart (@HaleyCarrots), and Mary Rezac (@MaryRezac).

What are you waiting for? Grab your phone and go!

GOD MADE LAUGHTER

by Sergio Bermudez

I know this seems to be a contradictory idea: that we're supposed to value the Church and her teachings above all things and yet we can dare to laugh at our faulty understanding of them. Well, there is an important distinction. Clearly, intention and who or what you're targeting is key in all this and something to be mindful of. It is a strange line to walk between what is sacred and the human error in understanding the sacred. There is plenty of space there for jokes.

For example, St. John XXIII once wrote, "There are three ways to face ruin: women, gambling, and farming. My father chose the most boring one."

Dissecting a joke is the least interesting thing you can do, but let's look at this a bit. The pope was obviously mocking the idea of sin, even the concept of family and all that. But he did it in a way that subverts the concept. His joke focused on human weakness. This might seem out of place from what we expect from a pope, but the reality is that Catholics have been joking and pushing ideas since the beginning. Contrary to the myth, not every Catholic is some uptight kid who only enjoys prayer and smiles a bit too widely for comfort.

In fact, many saints cultivated humor and understood that it's an important part of the human experience. St. Philip Neri once shaved half his beard—not to teach people or anything but simply because it was funny.

What does that have to do with making jokes about the Catholic Church? Well, to be honest, nothing. Although the Catholic has to be aware not to mock the Church, and certainly not the Divine, there is no set line of what is allowed and what isn't. Although there are times to be mindful of what is in good taste and what is in poor taste, and audience is key, there are no set-in-stone rules for what one must avoid at all times. We're all unique, and jokes simply have to be made carefully. A joke that elicits a laugh is a success of sorts, but a joke that causes polite laughter and a casual distancing may not be the goal. One cannot build friendships or understandings on outrage, and so charitable mockery must be done carefully. Although there is a time for mockery and a time for seriousness, it does not run on a schedule, and so one must find his or her own timing.

Now, I have taught you all I know about humor, so go forth and make your own jokes!

COOL SAINT: ST. THOMAS MORE

As the patron saint of lawyers, Thomas More certainly knew a bit about humor and joking around. He was a very well-known English lawyer, social philosopher, author, statesman, and noted Renaissance humanist back in his time. He stood up against the Protestant Reformation and fought back against the political establishment by writing a book titled *Utopia* about an imaginary ideal island.

He is best known for refusing to sign an Oath of Supremacy, which would have recognized King Henry VIII as head of the Church in England, and when you refuse to sign off on a guy like that, we all know what happens.

St. Thomas More was beheaded for treason in July 1535, canonized as a martyr in 1935, and declared the patron of statesman and politicians by Pope John Paul II in the year 2000.

St. Thomas More, pray for us!

FORGOTTEN PRAYER

Prayer for Good Humor

Grant me, O Lord, good digestion, and also something to digest.

Grant me a healthy body, and the necessary good humor to maintain it.

Grant me a simple soul that knows to treasure all that is good

and that doesn't frighten easily at the sight of evil,

but rather finds the means to put things back in their place.

Give me a soul that knows not boredom, grumblings, sighs and laments,

nor excess of stress, because of that obstructing thing called "I."

Grant me, O Lord, a sense of good humor.

Allow me the grace to be able to take a joke and to discover in life a bit of joy,

and to be able to share it with others.

—St. Thomas More

ACTIVITY

People are always up for making jokes at the expense of Catholics. The time has come for us to turn things around. There are plenty of hilarious jokes that relate to the faith and can even get a smile out of the most hardened secularist.

Get creative! You're the one trying to live an authentically Catholic life in a very post-Christian world. You know exactly how to find the humor in that struggle because you live it each and every day. Starting sharing the laughs with everyone you know.

WHAT ABOUT BEARDS?

by Fr. Kyle Schnippel

During the summer of 2014, as I was finishing an eight-year stint as vocation director for my home archdiocese and preparing to move full-time into life as a parish priest, I took the opportunity for an extended vacation. Two weeks to spend with friends and then family offered a much-needed break from the hectic life I was leading, a good chance to unplug from living downtown and readjust my schedule to the routine of the parish.

For most men on vacations (or at least as I remember my father doing when we were away), one of the easiest things to drop is the morning shave. Scruffy becomes the new way of things. (As a side note, I was not blessed with a full head of hair, so I normally keep a polished pate, as it were.)

After a few days, hmm. . . . *Let's see what we can do here* . . . I repolished the "chrome dome" and just trimmed up the sides to see how this newfound beard would look. Lo and behold, as I was hanging with some friends, I learned they thought it was cool. As it filled in over the next week or so, I was really glad to rock the "Jesus look" and gain some hipster cred with my close-cropped whiskers. (Despite a slight desire to grow out the gnarly "brewer's beard," the demands of the parish have me keeping it short.)

A year later, I had the opportunity to spend an extended period of time with NET Ministries during their fall training, when they prepare to send teams of young adults out around the country in vans to conduct retreat and evangelization work. During the initial retreat, priest alumni of NET are invited back to be witnesses of the power of the Spirit in these young people's lives and just to be around to minister to them.

One priest alumnus who returned that year was a member of the Conventual Franciscans of the Renewal based in New York City. Founded by Fr. Benedict Groeschel, C.F.R., in the mid-1980s, the order has a standing policy of the friars all having some sort of facial hair, and most of them wear the long, gnarly, bushy beards that are often associated with home and / or craft brewers today (and saints?).

Knowing this was their custom, we engaged in a long discussion about the importance of beards in the history of the Franciscan order and why the men continue to wear them today. The Capuchins (the C.F.R. priests and brothers were founded by eight Capuchins in 1988) broke away from the mainline Franciscans in the early to mid-1500s, a time of great opulence in the Church and in Europe. (This was also the time of the Protestant Reformation.) The great Age of Discovery was in full swing, and rival empires were set to carve up the newly discovered American territories.

As a sign of the opulence and wealth, men would stay either clean-shaven or wear neatly trimmed beards. It was a sign of luxury and ease to be able to afford the fineries that came with the clean look.

Combatting the look of opulence and wealth with that desire to return to the spirit of St. Francis's poverty, the Capuchins adopted as part of their Order a desire to have long, unkempt beards. They wanted to make themselves "ugly" in the fashions of the current day as a way of rejecting what was popular for the sake of Christ; and the longer and gnarlier the beards, the better!

This tradition continues to be handed down and lived out among Capuchin religious priests and brothers to this day; and many diocesan priests are adopting it as their own, as well, even though the tradition for "secular" clergy has typically been to be clean-shaven.

For many in the younger generation, the desire to share in this unkempt look is strong. It is a way of setting oneself apart from others and shunning the popular look of the day. For some, it makes them look older; for others, a beard lowers their apparent age. For those in the corporate world, it is a way to set oneself apart, too. And there is an aura of distinction and wisdom that comes from wearing the beard. After all, if it is good enough for Jesus, it is good enough for me, too!

Which brings this discussion to a rather important point: beards are biblical! In portraits of the Last Supper, Jesus and the apostles are all typically depicted with beards, except for John the Beloved, as tradition says he was still a teenager and so he is depicted clean-shaven. In the images on the Shroud of Turin and the Veil of Veronica, Jesus clearly has a beard.

But beards were biblical long before Jesus, too. The book of Leviticus commands, "Do not clip your hair at the temples, nor spoil the edges of your beard"(19:27). It seems a strange command to make, but it was a reminder that the people of Israel were different from their neighbors, and when the men looked at their images in a mirror, their beards were a sign that they were consecrated as the holy people of God. The instruction not to clip the hair at the temples is why, to this day, ultra-Orthodox Jews have those long curls framing their faces.

Certainly, today the law requiring a man to wear a beard is no longer in effect for Christians, but to do so is a good connection back to the very foundations of our faith as the nation of Israel was being formed as a people.

Interestingly, beards can even be a good hermeneutical tool for interpreting one of the more difficult verses in the narrative of the Old Testament. In 2 Samuel, chapter 11, we find the narrative of the sin of King David with Bathsheba, the wife of Uriah. (If someone says the Bible is boring, show that person this chapter!) It starts with a rather cryptic verse: "At the turn of the year, the time when kings go to war, David sent out Joab along with his officers and all Israel, and they laid waste the Ammonites and besieged Rabbah. David himself remained in Jerusalem." It's that second part, "the time when kings go to war," that really causes biblical scholars trouble.

At this point, there are a few important things to keep in mind:

- The Bible was not fully broken into chapters and verses until the 1500s.
- The authors of the various books of the Bible might have drawn from various sources, but they wrote the story out in one narrative thread.
- One of the first principles when trying to discern the meaning of a difficult passage is to check what lies before and after that particular passage.

With these three criteria in mind, look at 2 Samuel 10:1–5, from the chapter before the last excerpt:

> After this, the king of the Ammonites died, and Hanun his son succeeded him as king. David said, "I will show kindness to Hanun, the son of Nahash, as his father showed kindness to me." Therefore David sent his servants to Hanun to console him concerning his father. But when David's servants had entered the land of the Ammonites, the Ammonite princes said to their lord Hanun, "Do you think David is doing this—sending you these consolers—to honor your father? Is it not

rather to explore the city, to spy on it, and to overthrow it, that David has sent his servants to you?" So Hanun seized David's servants, shaved off half their beards, cut away the lower halves of their garments at the buttocks, and sent them away. David was told of it and he sent word for them to be intercepted, for the men had been greatly disgraced. "Remain at Jericho," the king told them, "until your beards have grown again; then come back here."(2 Sm 10:1–5)

In the rest of this passage from 2 Samuel, we see that the kingdom of David went to war for justice after the Ammonites shamed his servants—by shaving their beards. Isn't it interesting that beards were such an important sign of a man's dignity that kingdoms went to war over them? Through this story, we come to see the importance of our exterior appearance aligning with our interior values.

COOL SAINT: ST. PHILIP NERI

In light of David's servants having their beards half shorn, there could be no better saint to associate with a beard than St. Philip Neri. Born in Florence in 1515, he displayed a wicked sense of humor throughout his life. By 1533, he moved to Rome and continued his studies.

After forming a confraternity of laymen to help with pilgrims coming to Rome, he was convinced that he could do more as a priest and was ordained in 1551—his sense of humor still intact. His humor often became part of his teaching, too. When an associate asked if he could wear a hair shirt as a penance, Fr. Neri agreed, as long as it was on the outside of his clothes. The laughter and jokes directed at him would do more for his humility than any type of physical mortification.

He applied this humor to himself, as well. He was often found in ridiculous clothing, and he had a habit of shaving off half of his beard. He would use anything he could to engage others in conversations about God, and he found that laughter was the best tool he had to open these conversations.

But despite his love of humor, he took prayer very seriously and would often be taken into the heights of deep mystical prayer—so much so that it was difficult for him to celebrate Mass publicly because he would lose himself. After a long illness, he died in 1595, at the age of eighty.

FORGOTTEN PRAYER

The third of four Suffering Servant laments in the book of Isaiah, this one is a reminder that reading scripture itself can be a great source of prayer. Classically identified as pointing to Jesus Christ, the laments offer a wonderful opportunity for prayerful meditation during Lent and the approach to Holy Week.

> The Lord GOD has given me
>> a well-trained tongue,
> That I might know how to answer the weary
>> a word that will waken them.
> Morning after morning
>> he wakens my ear to hear as disciples do;
> The Lord GOD opened my ear;
>> I did not refuse,
>> did not turn away.
> I gave my back to those who beat me,
>> my cheeks to those who tore out my beard;
> My face I did not hide
>> from insults and spitting.
>
> The Lord GOD is my help,
>> therefore I am not disgraced;
> Therefore I have set my face like flint,

> knowing that I shall not be put to shame.
> He who declares my innocence is near.
>> Who will oppose me?
>> Let us appear together.
> Who will dispute my right?
>> Let them confront me.
> See, the Lord God is my help;
>> who will declare me guilty?
> See, they will all wear out like a garment,
>> consumed by moths.
> Who among you fears the Lord,
>> heeds his servant's voice?
> Whoever walks in darkness,
>> without any light,
> Yet trust in the name of the Lord
>> and rely upon their God! (Is 50:4–10)

ACTIVITY

How could it be anything else?

Grow. A. Beard!

And for our female readers: Encourage your male friends to grow beards! Oftentimes, a man can feel as if growing a beard isn't going to work for him (or that the women in his life will disapprove), but you never know until you try it out. Drop a casual hint about how cool it would be if he rocked the "Jesus look," and see if he takes your advice.

AND THEN THERE WERE SANDALS

by Mary Rezac

It was tough deciding on a shoe that truly represents the hipster Catholic. Many of us, including the original hipster Catholic, St. John Paul II, have rocked the Converse at some point in our lives.

Another option is Vans. I've always been more partial to Vans. There's something about the unexpectedness of someone like me, who is very much not a skateboarder, wearing these very-much-skater shoes that speaks to my always-bucking-the-norm hipster soul. Plus, they are super easy to slip on before heading out the door—still allowing me to make it to flag ceremony on time when I worked as a (non-Catholic) summer-camp counselor.

But if I could pinpoint a particular kind of footwear that truly unites us hipster Catholics, it would be the sandal. And the type of sandal selected by the wearer breaks us up into further subcultures.

Are you wearing Chacos or Tevas? Then you might work at Camp Wojtyla, Catholic Youth Expeditions, or some similar Catholic summer camp. Are you more of a Birkenstock kind of Catholic? Perhaps you're a seminarian, a priest, or an aspiring Discalced Carmelite.

As for me and my house, we always tended to favor the Birkenstocks (which we affectionately referred to as Birks—or, if paired with socks, then 'stocks 'n' socks). And when I say "my house," I'm talking about my college household, Avila, named after St. Teresa of Avila. The household in and of itself was an extremely hipster thing to be a part of, since I did not go to a Catholic or otherwise religious university. It was founded by five rogue women (not unlike Teresa herself) from the Newman Center who wanted to live in community even while off campus and to grow closer to the Lord. It often attracted the *hipsterest* of Catholic women as a result of this grassroots authenticity.

It was one of the most hipster of the six of us in the household, Caitlin, who kicked off the Birks trend (pun originally unintended but now deliberate). At the time, she was discerning with the Franciscan Sisters of the Renewal in New York, whose sandal-shod feet inspired her to wear brown Arizona-style Birkenstocks in most weather. She would shed her Birks in the chapel if she could at all do so without being too conspicuous. Many hipster Catholics started following Caitlin's example, and pretty soon, bare feet during adoration, at daily Mass, or on any terrain considered holy ground (see Exodus 3:5 and Acts 7:33) was not an uncommon sight at the Newman Center.

The rest of us in the house soon followed suit, wearing our Birks with shorts and dresses in the summertime, and our 'stocks 'n' socks with flannel plaid button-up shirts in the fall and winter (unless there was major snow on the ground). Add a scarf, and you've got the Avila hipster Catholic uniform.

Any hipster worth their (organic, non-GMO) salt rocks the granny cardigans or the grandpa suspenders at some point. Breaking supposed rules of fashion—wearing old people clothes, socks with sandals, scarves *ad nauseum*—is the bread and butter of the hipster life.

But there's something about the sandal that's uniquely hipster Catholic. I've often heard Birks referred to as "the Jesus sandal." Unless you've really not been paying attention to Catholic footwear, you'll have noticed that there's been a resurgence of Birkenstock in Catholics at large—priests and seminarians, hipster Catholic FOCUS missionaries, Totus Tuus teachers, religious sisters—they're popping up everywhere.

At one point, my pastor, having realized that he and I were wearing the exact same Birks, remarked, "My youth group kids told me those are old people shoes."

But Father's comment only further proves their hipster status; right?

There's also something about the sandal that's biblical, that implies a pilgrimage. They help you channel your inner apostle, so you can be like the ones whom Jesus sent out wearing sandals and just one tunic (see Mark 6:9). They imply simplicity of spirit and allow you to easily slip out of them if you encounter holy ground.

So the next time you're in a big group of Catholics, look down. Chances are you can spot the hipster Catholics by their sandals.

COOL SAINT:
ST. TERESA OF AVILA

It felt wrong to choose anyone but St. Teresa of Avila, whose obscureness I will argue for on account of my never having heard of her until college (although that may have been out of ignorance rather than actual obscurity, but I digress). She's also definitely the most obscure of what I call the "Trifecta of Teresas"—one is more likely to hear about St. Thérèse of Liseiux or St. Teresa of Calcutta than one is to hear about St. Teresa of Avila these days.

But most importantly, St. Teresa of Avila was the stubborn, norm-bucking reformer of probably the most recognizable shoeless, sandal-shod order in the Church: the Discalced (which means "de-shoed") Carmelites. When she began to realize how much the Carmelites were straying from a simple life of prayer, St. Teresa stubbornly went ahead with the founding of a new, reformed order, despite many difficulties from within and beyond her convent walls.

St. Teresa was also unafraid to be real with God, an authenticity highly valued by the hipster Catholic community. Perhaps the best illustration of this happened when, on her way to visit a convent, she was bucked off her horse and fell into a river. Complaining to God, she said, "If this is how you treat your friends, no wonder you have so few!"

She also enjoys the elite title of Doctor of the Church, a designation she shares with just three other women. If St. Teresa of Avila were alive today, she would definitely be among the ranks of hipster Catholics.

FORGOTTEN PRAYER

One of St. Teresa of Avila's better-known prayers is "Let Nothing Disturb Thee," but she has a lesser-known prayer (or poem) called "Christ Has No Body." I thought it was appropriate, because we've been talking about feet.

> Christ has no body now on earth but yours;
> no hands but yours; no feet but yours.
> Yours are the eyes through which he looks out with
> compassion on this world;
> yours are the feet with which he is to go about doing
> good;
> yours are the hands with which he is to bless men now.
> —St. Teresa of Avila

ACTIVITY

If you're a hipster Catholic, you probably remember the photo of Karol Wojtyla on a camping trip in the woods, his Converse-d foot casually propped up against a tree as he looks out at the wilderness. Since the future–Pope John Paul II embodied so much of the hipster Catholic spirit, here's how to have a hipster Catholic, JPII-inspired camping trip.

Whom to bring: friends who want to grow in their faith with you; friends whom you want to evangelize to; any priest you can get to agree to accompany you and say mountainside Mass.

What to bring: other than obvious camping essentials, your hipster Catholic sandals (Chacos work best here), a cord rosary that you don't mind getting wet or dirty, and an actual Breviary or Christian prayer book since your access to iBreviary will be cut off.

When to go: whenever you, your friends, and your recruited priest are free. Bonus points if it coincides with St. John Paul II's feast day. If camping sans priest over a weekend, be sure to check out local Mass times at MassTimes.org before heading out.

Where to go: as far away from people as possible but still close enough to a church, if necessary (see previous).

Why: Getting out into God's creation is one of the best ways to seek silence, to unplug from technology and all its distractions, and to focus on your relationship with the Lord and with others. Jesus often withdrew into creation by himself to pray, and mountains are frequently referenced as holy places in scripture—places where earth seems closer to heaven. Camping trips are also a phenomenal way for disciples to grow closer to each other in community—it was one of Karol Wojtyla's favorite things to do with his students in Poland before he was elected as pope. What could be more hipster Catholic than that?

THE GOOD IN VOCATIONAL ANGST

by Melissa Keating

I'm a single, midtwenties Catholic, which means the word *vocation* pops up in my news feed even more frequently than ignorant political rants. Unfortunately, unlike angry Facebook posts, those about vocation don't make me feel morally superior and intelligent compared to the person posting it. They just make me feel as if I'm being denied something.

Let me be clear: I believe that vocation is important. I get that it's under attack in a culture that cannot understand a healthy marriage between two people, let alone the spiritual marriage of religious life or priesthood. I am pro-vocation. I promise. It's just that sometimes in our quest to stress the importance of vocations, we make the mistake of equating them to accepting God's love. That is utter nonsense.

This became clear to me during my second summer as a FOCUS missionary. That was the summer my life fell apart and I stayed with a college roommate while I worked on my fundraising. Staying with her family was an immersion in Christian family life. It was a beautiful mess, difficult in all the best ways. I loved it.

But it was also really, really hard. Several of my friends got married that summer, and I couldn't afford to attend their weddings. Others entered religious life, and I couldn't attend their going-away parties. I was a hot mess sleeping in a friend's spare room while my good friends and peers started their vocations. It sucked. Being included in my friend's family's daily rhythm was healing, but it also made it painfully clear to me how unprepared I was to make a complete gift of myself in any situation. I didn't want to give myself away. I just wanted to be safe. But if vocation was God's plan for my life, shouldn't I be focusing on it? Wasn't that the next step as a disciple?

One night, I was drawn to the story of Jesus washing the disciples' feet in St. John's gospel. I prayed through it using the Ignatian method of prayer, which includes using your imagination to really enter into the scene. I used to joke with my students that it's like daydreaming or writing mental fanfiction about the Bible, but really, it's so much more. It's trusting that God can use your imagination to communicate just as much as he can use your hands to relieve someone else's suffering. It requires careful discernment and humility (you're not adding to the doctrine of the Church; you're just talking to Jesus, and you better check with someone holier than you before you take anything too seriously). But if you enter deep into the prayer, there comes a point where things start happening that don't come from you. Again, you have to carefully discern the source of these movements, but Ignation prayer is worth learning just to be able to have this time with Jesus.[4]

In this prayer, I was helping to prepare the Last Supper. St. John, my patron saint, led me to the Upper Room, where I stood in the back and held a basin of water. I watched as the other disciples and Jesus entered the room and then sat down to eat. As I read the story, the phrase "loved . . . to the end" from John 13:1 especially stood out to me. So as they ate, I watched Jesus interact with his apostles. I was filled with wonder and ache at how much he loved them even as he knew the suffering he was about to endure. I saw St. John accept that love, accept it so deeply that it became his identity, so that he couldn't leave

Jesus, even when almost everyone else did. I watched him rest his head on Jesus' breast. I wanted to learn from him.

When the meal ended, Jesus came to me. His eyes and the way he looked at me did not come from my imagination. He held me close, one hand tangled in my hair and the other rubbing small circles on my back. I just breathed and cried and listened to his heart beat as he held me. I experienced more healing in that moment than I had in a month of emoting. Then he offered me his hand and led me back to the table. We knelt together and washed the feet of the apostles one by one. I took in the discomfort and amazement of each apostle's face—from St. Peter's blustering to Judas's quiet tolerance. I didn't speak; I just served with Christ.

When we reached the end, I moved to wash Jesus' feet. He held my hand and shook his head no. St. John lifted me into a sitting position, and held my hand while Jesus began to wash my feet. I was really scared, but St. John put his arm around me and Jesus looked at me again. Then I saw the whole picture through their eyes. They had invited me to dinner, and I stood in the back and tried to manage it all. I had tried to earn Jesus' love, and he ran his fingers through my hair and washed my feet. *Loved to the end.* He loves me so much. My heart felt as if it was breaking because of how much I loved him back. Instead of trying to prove my love, I sat there and let him heal me.

Other people were coming in and out of the chapel during this, and I was frequently distracted by trying to hide how hard I was crying. Yet the look on Jesus' face is burned into my memory. When the prayer was over, I thanked him for a few minutes and then went out to my car. I turned on my stereo, and a song came on I had never heard before. It couldn't have just been a coincidence. I started to cry all over again as I realized this song, which could so easily be used to describe marital love, was Jesus speaking directly to me.

So that's my vocation: being loved and loving. It's not to figure out which vows I'm supposed to take. Like my patron saint, my life's purpose is to let Christ's love replace even my own identity. Through that acceptance, his love will spread to others. He may become more specific about how he wants this to happen, but it's unchristian to say that he isn't at work in my life because I don't have a wedding ring or a wimple.

We need to claim this. Never in history have we, as a Church, had a better understanding of the fact that Christ wants every last one of us to be completely and irrevocably *his*. We effectively tell him that his love isn't enough when we unconsciously decide that we aren't real Christian adults because we don't have a vowed vocation. Of course we have everything we need to live a life rooted in love from and for him. He's not holding back, so why do we?

COOL SAINT: BL. MARCEL CALLO

If you want to learn more about the vocation to love and be loved, I highly recommend learning about Bl. Marcel Callo, a French Catholic who was conscripted to serve in World War II but showed his brothers and sisters in Christ true love by continuing to engage in Christian activities that eventually led to his imprisonment and death.

FORGOTTEN PRAYER

This prayer is attributed to St. Francis Xavier on iPieta (but it rhymes really well in English, which makes me suspicious):

> My God, I love thee, not because
> I hope for heaven thereby,
> Nor yet since they who love Thee not
> Must burn eternally.
> Thou, O my Jesus, Thou didst me
> Upon the Cross embrace

For me didst bear the nails and spear
And manifold disgrace;
And griefs and torments numberless,
And sweat of agony;
E'en death itself; and all for one
Who was Thine enemy.
Then why, O blessed Jesus Christ,
Should I not love Thee well,
Not for the sake of winning Heaven,
Or of escaping Hell;
Not with the hope of gaining aught,
Not seeking a reward;
But as Thyself has loved me,
O ever-loving Lord?
E'en so I love Thee, and will love
And in Thy praises sing,
Solely because Thou art my God,
And my eternal King.

Also, I would love if y'all would say a prayer for the McAwesome family.

ACTIVITY

Try Ignatian meditation!

Pick a story from one of the gospels. Read through it once. Then take a few minutes and let yourself quiet down. Thank God for all of the blessings he has given you, and give the time to him. Ask him for any specific graces you'd like for this time in prayer. Then begin to move through the passage slowly, taking time to experience it in your imagination. See the people and places. Hear their words, and feel the fabric of their clothes. Smell the dirt of the street or the fruit in a merchant's cart. Try becoming a character in the story.

If a jarring or unpleasant thought comes to you, don't dwell on it. You can decide later if that was really God speaking to you. For now, just enter the story. When you're done, talk to him about what you experienced for a while. Then thank him for the time in prayer (even if it seemed unfruitful), and write down any realizations or resolutions.

THE LOCAL CRAFT
[CATHOLIC?] BREWERY SCENE

by Sarah Vabulas

In a world where more people are turning away from religion, we practicing Catholics are called to live the New Evangelization in different ways. As lay men and women living out in the world, we are called to reach people whom the Church wouldn't otherwise reach. Pope Francis does this really well with his outward living of the Christian Gospel through visiting the infirm and the poor on a regular basis. This also means reaching out to noncatechized people around us. Believe it or not, not everyone around us has heard the Good News of the Gospel.

This is why I believe we can reach the hearts of our neighbors with basic things such as food, sports, and even beer. God is present in all things. I like to tell the story of how beer saved the world. But the truth is, Catholic monks saved the world by giving beer to the people! In the Middle Ages, water was unclean, and access to clean drinking water was scarce. However, fermented beverages such as beer and wine were safe to drink. So Catholic monks brewed beer and used it to evangelize and keep people from drinking dirty water. We don't need to do the same now, but we can use beer as a stepping-stone to share the faith.

It is only natural that good conversations arise at a pub or at a local brewery. It is a time of great joy and merriment, as we enjoy the fruit of human labor. With God present in all things, it is a good opportunity to evangelize, even at the brewery. I love visiting breweries and sampling their wide variety of styles. Often I am asked how I know so much about beer, and I begin to tell about my journey into sampling beer and home brewing. The question always arises about my blog and my book, giving me the opportunity to share my passion for a good brew and for the good Lord.

In all that I do, I keep in mind my favorite verse from scripture: "For I am not ashamed of the Gospel. It is the power of God for the salvation of everyone who believes" (Rom 1:16).

Real-life hipsters love a good craft beer. In fact, many people blame the surge of craft beer on the hipster movement (that and the surge in price of Pabst Blue Ribbon). It's only natural that Catholic hipsters and secular hipsters could blend so well together at a brewery. After all, Catholic monks make some of the best beers in the entire world!

I am also a home brewer and find this is another great way to share the truth of the Gospel. I name all my beers after saints or words relating to the Catholic Church, so when I share my beer with others, it's an opportunity for me to evangelize in small ways. I also try to live by the precept of the Benedictine Order of monks: *ora et labora*. Prayer and work. In all that I do, may I work hard and share the Gospel through it.

Never underestimate the power of the Gospel and what vessel the Holy Spirit will use to spread the Word. It can be through small things like beer if you say yes to God and allow him to work within you.

COOL SAINT: ST. BENEDICT

St. Benedict lived in Nursia, an Umbrian town, in about 480. He journeyed to Rome to finish his studies when he was a late teen and there decided to give up the world and live in community and prayer. Later in his life, he wrote the Rule that many monks, including the beer-brewing monks of today, live under.

Benedict died on March 21, 543. It is said he died with high fever on the very day God told him he would. He is the patron saint of Europe and students. His feast day is celebrated on July 11.

FORGOTTEN PRAYER

Novena to St. Benedict

Glorious Saint Benedict, sublime model of virtue, pure vessel of God's grace! Behold me humbly kneeling at your feet. I implore you in your loving kindness to pray for me before the throne of God. To you I have recourse in the dangers that daily surround me. Shield me against my selfishness and my indifference to God and to my neighbor. Inspire me to imitate you in all things. May your blessing be with me always, so that I may see and serve Christ in others and work for his kingdom. Graciously obtain for me from God those favors and graces which I need so much in the trials, miseries, and afflictions of life. Your heart was always full of love, compassion, and mercy toward those who were afflicted or troubled in any way. You never dismissed without consolation and assistance anyone who had recourse to you. I therefore invoke your powerful intercession, confident in the hope that you will hear my prayers and obtain for me the special grace and favor I earnestly implore. (*Mention your petition.*)

Help me, great Saint Benedict, to live and die as a
faithful child of God, to run in the sweetness of his loving will, and to attain the eternal happiness of heaven.
Amen.[5]

ACTIVITY

Taste all the Trappist ales!

Invite your friends, Catholic and non-Catholic alike, for a
Trappist ale gathering. Purchase all the official Trappist beers,
and have a tasting party, discussing the thoughts of G. K. Chesterton (a great Catholic writer of the early twentieth century
and lover of all things beer) and the latest teachings from the
Holy Father. Enjoy the fruits of the labors of the monks, and
thank God for the gift of beer.

DISCOVER TUNES OUTSIDE THE MAINSTREAM

by Melissa Keating

I get the appeal of Christian music. We all love music. All of our lives are better if we memorize scripture and enhance our ability to pray always. It's just that everything on the Christian music channel is utterly predictable, and I think my soul would be better off if I had an audiobook of *The Da Vinci Code* running through my head continuously.

But I don't think we should just eradicate Christian music. After all, music is part of how we spread culture. It's a powerful form of communication and art. So I think we should all just be really picky and belligerent and demand that Christian artists do an insanely good job.

Much like Noah's family among the human race version 1.0, there are a few good bands to be found in this unrighteous genre. Here are my favorites, which will probably be hopelessly out of touch by the time this book is published.

- Luke Spehar—In addition to being an all-around cool dude, Luke just gets it. His music is deep and soulful and clearly flows from a mix of tons of practice and talent and a deep prayer life.

- Josh Garrels—He's our Beyoncé. He could commit a heinous crime and we, as a culture, would excuse him because his music is so perfect. Unlike Beyoncé, he sings beautiful songs about creation, the crucifixion, and true love. Start with "Farther Along."

- Run River North—They put the millennial soul to music. Check out "Growing Up," and then join me in campaigning to make it our generational anthem.

- The Oh Hellos—Fun fact: every Catholic received the charism of loving them at Confirmation, provided the sacrament took place before 2010 (2008 for Denver and Seattle dwellers).

- Needtobreathe—I know calling them hipster is a stretch, but I'm not going to punish them for being successful. They've made it for a reason. Best of all, they make the kind of music that reaches secular culture. I have actually heard one of their songs playing while I tried on jeans at H&M. Also, I needed to include at least one band that doesn't have what my friend Steve the Missionary calls that "Denver sound."

- Future of Forestry—I'm 90 percent sure they don't exist anymore, but they're too hipster to show up reliably on web search engines. They even transcend labels like "together" or "touring ever again." "Slow Your Breath Down" is one of my go-to calm down and focus on Jesus songs, and "Sanctiatis" is a fusion of Gregorian chant and electronic music that somehow works.

- Rivers and Robots—Honestly, I think most of their stuff sounds like generic Christian music, but they have one song that gets them on the list. It's called "The Bridegroom," and it's perfect. I especially recommend listening to it while driving through the Rocky Mountains at sunset with Mary Rezac after an accidental trip to New Mexico. Or, you know, while running on your treadmill. Whatever works.

- Jenny and Tyler—I once spent an entire summer listening only to their music, and it didn't get old. They kind of remind me of The Civil Wars but better, because Jesus.

- The Crossroads Pursuit—I have been assured they will put more of their music online before this book is published, so you're welcome, world. My iPod is doing this thing where it jumps to "Ash Wednesday" every time I turn it on, and I think it might be my guardian angel doing me a favor.

OTHER CHRISTIAN ARTISTS I LOVE

- Lev
- Mike Mangione
- Seeker and Servant
- Rend Collective
- The Brilliance
- Penny and Sparrow
- Audrey Assad
- Hildegard of Bingen

I can't call the following artists and songs Catholic, but I've meditated on them during Holy Hour:

- Mumford and Sons (obviously)
- Perry West
- Vance Joy (My mess *is* yours, Jesus!)
- Josh Groban (again, obviously)
- "Let It Go" from the *Frozen* soundtrack (detachment from sin)
- "Closing Time" by Semisonic (weirdly perfect when you apply it to life as mission)
- "This Kind of Love" by Sister Hazel (listen to this while looking at the Eucharist and don't cry, I dare you)
- "Endless Night" followed by "He Lives in You" from Broadway's *The Lion King* (laugh all you want, but pull these out next time you're in desolation)
- Lord Huron and ABBA (two very different bands, but they both possess the kind of transcendental beauty that lifts your soul right to God)

COOL SAINT:
ST. HILDEGARD OF BINGEN

St. Hildegard of Bingen was a German Benedictine abbess, writer, composer, philosopher, mystic, visionary, and polymath (look that one up!). She is considered to be the founder of scientific natural history in Germany, and her music continues to be popular down to this very day.

FORGOTTEN PRAYER

O Lord God, will to give me
All that leads me to you.
O Lord God, take away from me
All that diverts me from you.
O Lord God, take me, also, from myself
And give me completely to yourself.

—St. Nicholas of Flue

ACTIVITY

Christian music bingo: Take out your bingo card, and point your favorite streaming music app to the Christian music station. Mark the appropriate space when any of the following occur. Ready to see how quickly you get a bingo?

B1: Gospel choir comes in at the end
B2: "on my knees"
B3: "consuming fire"
B4: male singing high alto
B5: improperly conjugated verb in the singer's native language

I1: "my heart's desire"
I2: eucharistic language used by a band that doesn't believe in Real Presence
I3: "all nations/every nation/each nation/nations"

I4: hook that requires a kick drum and is frequently played during Communion

I5: "mercy like rain"

N1: "the Supper of the Lamb"

N2: "when he rolls up his sleeves he ain't just putting on the Ritz"

N3: free space (use for switches to live recordings of crowds singing along)

N4: "guard your/my heart" sans explanation of what this phrase means

N5: catch yourself doing hand motions

G1: "your Church"

G2: reference to some form of maritime waters

G3: unexpected reference to death and entropy without mention of redemption

G4: surprising collective noun (i.e., "brood of vipers")

G5: "righteousness"

O1: quotes attributed to Jesus that he never said

O2: remembering an old lady at Mass rocking out to this song

O3: "whoooooooaaaaa" (basically a free space)

O4: something about chains or bonds (kinky versions on normal radio don't count)

O5: song you actually like (JK, it's a free space)

Thanks for playing!

PART TWO
REDISCOVER THE STUFF

The smells and bells.

From an outside perspective, the Catholic faith often can seem a little weird with all the "stuff" our faith contains. From holy water to liturgical dress to rosaries to scapulars, we have to admit that there's definitely apparent evidence to back up this complaint.

What those on the outside don't understand, however, is the reason behind all the stuff. Catholics have a sacramental way of looking at the world, and that logically leads to our seeing things quite a bit differently from our non-Catholic Christian brothers and sisters. As it says in paragraph 1131 of the *Catechism of the Catholic Church*, "The visible rites by which the sacraments are celebrated signify and make present the graces proper to each sacrament."

Even beyond the sacraments, God uses the things of this world to draw our attention to something bigger: holy water to remind us that Jesus offers us cleansing from our sins, liturgical dress to connect us to the fact that we are a part of something bigger than our local parishes, scapulars to help us feel a reminder of our calling to holiness as we go about our regular day. It's all about drawing our attention to God and his plan for us as we continue to make our way through this busy and messy life.

So, let's get back into the stuff that gets us back into him!

DISPUTED DESTINATION

by Matt Dunn

You think it's "My Look"
Revealing my faith to all,
But it points inside.

TAKE A FRESH LOOK AT THAT ROSARY

by Tommy Tighe

As long as I can remember, I have carried a rosary around in my pocket. Not that I've always been dedicated to praying it, mind you, but something felt right about having it on me at all times just in case. As a naturally anxious person, I tend to picture myself getting into some sort of calamity where I would need to pull it out for prayers in the face of impending death, and because of that, I make sure never to leave home without it.

My relationship with the Rosary took a drastic turn upon the death of my mother when I was just twenty-three years old. I was so angry at God for allowing the loss of my mom, and that anger was most likely palpable to all those trying to console me. Early on, their heartfelt efforts proved unfruitful, and my anger raged on until the Rosary service on the night before her funeral.

I'm not sure exactly what happened, but during the recitation of the Rosary, I felt an incredible calm and peace pour over me. Despite all that was going on, as I joined in each Our Father and each Hail Mary, I felt consoled. I felt as if the Blessed Mother was taking care of my mother and taking care of me in the most comforting way possible.

From that point forward, the rosary in my pocket became much more than something I just grabbed and carried along with my keys and spare change; it became my primary means of reaching out to God in prayer.

As a Catholic hipster, of course, I wasn't content simply to embrace my newfound devotion and leave it at that. Instead, I took some time to delve into the deep spirituality contained within this 2,000-year-old Church in an effort to find prayers a little more off the beaten path:

- The Servite Rosary—A Rosary that was given to us through the Servite Order, focusing our meditation on the Seven Sorrows of Mary.
- The Chaplet of St. Michael—An awesome prayer that helps us to connect with the fact that the choirs of angels are very real and very ready to help us in our moments of need.
- The Divine Mercy Chaplet—A more well-known Rosary-type devotion given to us by St. Faustina, which focuses on the limitless mercy of Jesus' unconditional love.
- The Little Crown of the Blessed Virgin Mary—A chaplet that is promoted through St. Louis de Montfort's Total Consecration to Jesus through Mary and typically said by followers of that devotion on a daily basis.

There are many more Rosary-type prayers out there, and you only have to do a little searching to dig up one that speaks to you. Our Lady is willing, ready, and able to help us; all we have to do is pull that rosary out of our pocket and ask.

COOL SAINT:
ST. BRIDGET OF SWEDEN

St. Bridget was a mystic and founder of the Bridgettine nuns and monks. She experienced visions of Jesus beginning at the age of ten, and her visions included the Nativity of Jesus,

purgatory, and Jesus hanging on the Cross. She was also influential in the spread of the Seven Sorrows devotion.

St. Bridget of Sweden, pray for us.

FORGOTTEN PRAYER

First Prayer of St. Bridget of Sweden

O Jesus Christ! Eternal Sweetness to those who love
Thee, joy surpassing all joy and all desire, Salvation
and Hope of all sinners, Who hast proved that Thou
hast no greater desire than to be among men, even
assuming human nature at the fullness of time for the
love of men, recall all the sufferings Thou hast endured
from the instant of Thy conception, and especially
during Thy Passion, as it was decreed and ordained
from all eternity in the Divine plan. Remember, O
Lord, that during the Last Supper with Thy disciples,
having washed their feet, Thou gavest them Thy Most
Precious Body and Blood, and while at the same time
Thou didst sweetly console them, Thou didst foretell
them Thy coming Passion. Remember the sadness and
bitterness which Thou didst experience in Thy Soul as
Thou Thyself bore witness saying: "My Soul is sorrowful even unto death."

Remember all the fear, anguish and pain that Thou
didst suffer in Thy delicate Body before the torment of
the crucifixion, when, after having prayed three times,
bathed in a sweat of blood, Thou wast betrayed by
Judas, Thy disciple, arrested by the people of a nation
Thou hadst chosen and elevated, accused by false
witnesses, unjustly judged by three judges during the
flower of Thy youth and during the solemn Paschal
season.

Remember that Thou wast despoiled of Thy garments and clothed in those of derision; that Thy Face and Eyes were veiled, that Thou wast buffeted, crowned with thorns, a reed placed in Thy Hands, that Thou was crushed with blows and overwhelmed with affronts and outrages. In memory of all these pains and sufferings which Thou didst endure before Thy Passion on the Cross, grant me before my death true contrition, a sincere and entire confession, worthy satisfaction and the remission of all my sins. Amen.

ACTIVITY

Grab that rosary off of your rearview mirror, and start praying it! Many people complain that their minds tend to wander during the Rosary. They find it nearly impossible to stay focused on contemplating the mysteries while saying the prayers and moving the beads through their fingers. A great way to get focused is to pray the Scriptural Rosary.

Here's an example, going with the First Joyful Mystery: the Annunciation. Before each Hail Mary, reflect on the accompanying scripture verse:

- The angel Gabriel was sent from God . . . to a virgin betrothed to a man named Joseph, of the house of David, and the virgin's name was Mary. (Lk 1:26–27)
- [The angel] said, "Hail, favored one! The Lord is with you." (Lk 1:28)
- She was greatly troubled at what was said and pondered what sort of greeting this might be. Then the angel said to her, "Do not be afraid, Mary, for you have found favor with God." (Lk 1:29–30)
- "Behold, you will conceive in your womb and bear a son, and you shall name him Jesus. He will be great and will be called

Son of the Most High, . . . and of his kingdom there will be no end." (Lk 1:31–33)

- Mary said to the angel, "How can this be, since I have no relations with a man?" And the angel said to her in reply, "The holy Spirit will come upon you, and the power of the Most High will overshadow you. Therefore the child to be born will be called holy, the Son of God." . . . Mary said, "Behold, I am the handmaid of the Lord. May it be done according to your word." Then the angel departed from her. (Lk 1:34–35, 38)

O SCAPULAR, MY SCAPULAR

by Sarah Vabulas

I have a particular devotion to the Catholic practice of wearing a holy scapular. When I was growing up, my mom wore a gold chain with a medal around it. I always knew it was a religious necklace but wasn't truly certain of its meaning or significance. As I grew older, I began to ask about it and what this devotion meant to her. The Sacred Heart of Jesus appeared on one side, while a beautiful image of Mary appeared on the other. I too wanted to partake in this devotion.

I remember receiving my scapular medal in eighth or ninth grade, right around the time of my Confirmation. Pope John Paul II had blessed it, and I have worn it almost constantly—with several pauses for other girlie necklaces or religious symbols—since that day. It is part of my daily wardrobe. Because I wear it so often, I have been asked many times about its significance. This gives me a beautiful way to tell people about the relationship between Jesus and Mary and why we, as Christians, can and should honor our Blessed Mother the way the Catholic Church does.

A scapular is what some Catholics may call spiritual armor. The intent behind wearing a scapular is that the wearer, should he or she die while wearing it, receives special graces and indulgences in order to get to heaven. There are many types of scapulars, but the brown scapular belonging to the Carmelite Order of religious is the most popular.

For me, wearing my scapular is a daily reminder of my call to live a Christian life. It is a reminder of my humanity and how much I need Jesus in my heart, a reminder for me to honor our Lord and Savior by honoring his Mother. I know that my devotion to Mary and Jesus in this way has helped me to live a grace-filled life and to continue to say yes to God's plan. My scapular helps me to say no to evil and protects me from the wickedness that the devil stands for.

Many religious orders require a scapular (from *scapulae*, Latin for "shoulder blade") as part of the habit of religious men and women, and they wear the scapular as an apron. This tradition began with the Benedictines but has since moved into most religious communities today.

However, laypeople wanted to partake in this practice, and over time, the scapular was developed into what we know it to be today: a sacramental object made of two small panels of woven wool (the required material), each roughly two inches by three inches and connected by a loop of string. The scapular is worn with one panel resting over the breast and the other in approximately the same position on the back.

Tradition of the scapular states that a person who wears it should wear it devoutly. This means that one must try to remain in a state of grace (go to Confession often!), be properly enrolled into the scapular by a Catholic priest, and pray either the Little Office of the Blessed Virgin Mary or five decades of the Rosary daily. It's not just about wearing it, but rather it's a reminder to live a life pointed toward Jesus.

Pope John Paul II, believed to have worn a brown scapular since he was a boy, insisted that doctors not remove his scapular during surgery following the assassination attempt in May 1981. Fr. Mariano Cera, a Carmelite priest, told *Inside the Vatican* magazine, "Just before the Holy Father was operated on, he told the doctors, 'Don't take off the scapular.' And the surgeons left it on."[6] In his message to the Carmelites at the 750th anniversary of the bestowal of the scapular, Pope John Paul II said those who wear the scapular—or habit, as he called it—dedicate themselves to the service of our Lady for the good of the whole Church. The pontiff said, "Devotion to her cannot be limited to prayers and tributes in her honor on certain occasions, but must become a 'habit,' that is, a permanent orientation of one's own Christian conduct, woven of prayer and interior life, through frequent reception of the sacraments and the concrete practice of the spiritual and corporal works of mercy."[7]

COOL SAINT: ST. SIMON STOCK

Carmelite tradition says that the Blessed Virgin Mary appeared to St. Simon Stock at Cambridge, England, in 1251, answering his appeal for help for his oppressed order. There, Mary recommended the brown scapular to the Order of Our Lady of Mount Carmel and made promises of protection to all those who piously wore it. This apparition is under much argument now, but the tradition of the scapular remains. The scapular serves as a sign for all Carmelites of Mary's motherly protection and as a reminder of their personal commitment to follow Jesus in all that they do.

FORGOTTEN PRAYER

Procedure for Blessing and Investiture

Priest: Show us, O Lord, Thy mercy.

Respondent: And grant us Thy salvation.

P: Lord, hear my prayer.

R: And let my cry come unto Thee.

P: The Lord be with you.

R: And with your Spirit.

P: Lord Jesus Christ, Savior of the human race, sanctify by Thy power these scapulars, which for love of Thee and for love of Our Lady of Mount Carmel, Thy servants will wear devoutly, so that through the intercession of the same Virgin Mary, Mother of God, and protected against the evil spirit, they persevere until death in Thy grace. Thou who lives and reigns world without end. Amen.

The priest sprinkles with holy water the scapular and the person(s) being enrolled. He then invests person(s), saying:

P: Receive this blessed scapular and beseech the Blessed Virgin that through her merits, you may wear it without stain. May it defend you against all adversity and accompany you to eternal life. Amen.

After investiture the priest continues with the prayers:

P: I, by the power vested in me, admit you to participate in all the spiritual benefits obtained through the mercy of Jesus Christ by the Religious Order of Mount Carmel. In the name of the Father and of the Son and of the Holy Spirit. Amen.

May God Almighty, the Creator of heaven and earth, bless you, He who has deigned to join you to the

Confraternity of the Blessed Virgin of Mount Carmel; we beseech her to crush the head of the ancient serpent so that you may enter into possession of your eternal heritage through Christ our Lord.

R: Amen.

The priest then sprinkles again with holy water the person(s) enrolled.[8]

ACTIVITY

Obtain and wear a scapular!

Log on to your favorite Catholic store website, or drive over to your local Catholic bookstore, and purchase a scapular for your family and yourself. Then call your parish priest and invite him over for a meal and a home blessing, and ask him to invest upon you and your family the scapulars. Allow this to deepen your prayer life in new ways, asking God to bless you daily with the reminder of what you wear on your shoulders.

THE MUST-HAVE APPS

by Lisa M. Hendey

Scribes in Jesus' time had papyrus scrolls. Monks in the Middle Ages created and employed their illuminated manuscripts. My parents' generation memorized the *Baltimore Catechism*.

And I have my iPhone.

Part lifeline to my loved ones, part organizational wizard, my smartphone has also become one of my go-to prayer resources. Many of the tools I employ on a daily basis are Catholic apps, explicitly created by Catholic designers with the goal of helping us make daily prayer, service, and sharing of our gifts an organic part of the rest of our uber-wired lives.

Some of my favorite Catholic apps include these:

- The Pope App—While Pope Francis isn't the first Holy Father to have tweeted, he is the first to have his own official app. I'll often crack open the Pope App, created by the Vatican, simply to watch the live webcam views of six different hotspots in and around St. Peter's and imagine that I'm praying there. The app features all of the latest news from Rome, Pope Francis's tweets and official texts, video recaps, and much more. Plus—and this is a big plus from the Church that's still rocking parchment background on its home page—the app looks great!

- USA Catholic Church—This tool from the USCCB is an essential part of my morning prayer routine. I use it to access and pray with the daily Mass readings. I keep tabs on what Pope Francis is up to with the app's listings of news, photos, videos, and most importantly, the pontiff's amazing tweets. I even add national Catholic events such as the March for Life to my digital calendar. Even if I can't be at these events, I pray in solidarity with those in attendance.
- Mary—There are lots of Rosary apps out there, but I love the Marian app from the Marians of the Immaculate Conception. The app teaches about Marian doctrine and devotion, gives a timeline of Mary's role and history in the Church, and offers a cavalcade of Marian devotions. Pray the Rosary or a variety of chaplets. Learn about Marian Consecration. Check out Marian sacramentals, and learn new and classic prayers devoted to our Lady. After you've fallen in love with this app, check out the Divine Mercy app, also from the Marians.
- Rice Bowl—Some people think that Catholic Relief Services' Rice Bowl is just that little cardboard box that you stick on your table during the Lenten season. True Catholic hipsters rock the CRS Rice Bowl app on their smartphones all year long. The goal of this app is to make it easy for us to pray, fast, and give to the many worthy programs CRS has in place around the world. The Rice Bowl app simplifies incorporating Lenten prayer into my daily routine, and it also reminds me to keep the spirit of my Lenten devotions alive all year long. I love that I can safely and securely add virtual funds to my Rice Bowl to be donated at the end of Lent. I often find myself stopping prior to an impulse buy, pulling up the app, and reminding myself that the money for that tenth pair of flip-flops I was about to purchase can instead be donated through CRS to families around the world. The Rice Bowl app may be purple, but it is awesome all year long.
- Laudate—Every time I open the Laudate app, I'm overwhelmed by the expansive content it contains. Use it to pray in Latin or

English, devote yourself to the Liturgy of the Hours, watch EWTN, read multiple versions of the Bible, or end your day with an examen as you prepare for Confession.

Not all of my essential spiritual apps are explicitly Catholic. The following tools are part of my faith arsenal on a daily basis:

- Evernote—I use this virtual notebook for a variety of prayer-related purposes. My Evernote files contain my daily spiritual reflections on the gospel readings, my annual and monthly faith-related resolutions, lists of prayer intentions, spiritual books to read, and even a note to help me prepare for Confession.
- Instagram—Can a social media app be a spiritual tool? I say yes. With Instagram, I find new and creative ways not only to share my faith with online connections but also to grow in my faith. I follow a variety of priests, religious communities, and dioceses around the world and enjoy their frequent teaching posts. But I also learn quite a lot from lay men and women who use this daily photo-sharing app to let their joy for life and love and their relationship with Christ shine through in a variety of filtered hues.
- Twitter—I love Twitter for a variety of reasons, but most of all because at least a few times per week, I receive a 140-character-or-less homily from my Holy Father. Pope Francis can honestly say more in one tweet than many priests I know can say in a seven-minute homily. Another reason I love Twitter is the capacity to pray instantaneously with and for folks, especially when major catastrophes happen. Just as Twitter often takes us immediately to firsthand perspectives on world news, it enables us to pray directly for those most in need on a real-time basis.

Part of effectively using apps and smartphones as a must-have part of our spiritual life is also knowing when to put them away. As much as I love my apps, I try to force myself to power off my phone when at Mass or adoration. Unlike many of my friends, I have discovered that I lack the ability to ignore all of the push notifications that descend upon me when I have my phone in hand. As a result, you're more likely to see me holding actual rosary beads or even counting my God-given digits than using a Rosary app in our adoration chapel. It's great to know that I've got the app to pray with in my Mini Cooper at the start of a road trip. But it's also great to silence technology in the midst of life's craziness and simply be in the astounding presence of the greatest Designer the world has ever known.

COOL SAINT: ST. ELIGIUS

St. Eligius probably would have been an app designer had he lived in modern times. This patron saint of toolmakers was born near Limoges, France, around 590. A priest and later a bishop, Eligius was also a skilled metalworker. Known for his goldsmithing artistry, Eligius was a trusted advisor to the king and used his access to win alms for those most in need. Also the patron of sick horses and gas-station workers, St. Eligius is a terrific go-to intercessor for those of us who want to effectively employ digital tools in our spiritual lives and in the New Evangelization.

FORGOTTEN PRAYER

Daily morning prayer enables us to give the first fruits of our days to God. Praying at the start of the day equips us for whatever lies ahead and reminds us to offer the best of our work for God's greater glory.

Allegiance Prayer

Dear God in heaven, I pledge my allegiance to you. I give you my life, my work, and my heart. In turn, give me the grace of obeying your every direction to the fullest possible extent.

Morning Offering

O Jesus, through the Immaculate Heart of Mary, I offer you the prayers, works, joys, and sufferings of this day, for all the intentions of your Sacred Heart, in union with the Holy Sacrifice of the Mass throughout the world, in reparation for my sins, and for the intentions of the Holy Father. Amen.

ACTIVITY

What indispensable apps have greatly blessed your spiritual life? Have you taken stock of apps that cause you needless distraction or wasted time? Do an app audit this week, and organize your phone or tablet screens. Create folders for your highest-yield spiritual tools. Delete at least three time busters or spirit sappers. Commit to sharing your favorite religious app with your online friends as a means of sharing your faith. And last—but definitely the one activity that will earn you time off in purgatory—spend thirty minutes this week with an elderly friend or relative and help him or her learn something new on a smartphone or tablet.

HIPSTER THEOLOGY

by Sarah Vabulas

It doesn't get much more hipster than the Doctors of the Church. Currently we have thirty-six sainted, holy people who are called Doctors of the Church. It is believed that their writings are inspired by the Holy Spirit and therefore worthy of great study and reading.

I began to study St. Thomas Aquinas when I was in college. A Catholic friar who can write at length about many faith topics, including five arguments for the existence of God, is the epitome of a hipster Catholic. I enjoyed my study of Aquinas so much that I took two semesters of classes on his works in order to have a deeper understanding of the heart of his writings and what he had to say. That said, I am pretty sure I could study Aquinas for years and never fully comprehend the profound depth of his writings. The *Summa Theologica* changed my faith life.

Looking to St. Thérèse of Lisieux, another Doctor of the Church, we can learn about deep spirituality and how to have an intimate relationship with Jesus Christ on a simple and straightforward path.

Beyond the Doctors, there are many amazing books to read about the lives of our saints—from ones they wrote themselves to books others have written about their lives. Being a true Catholic hipster means finding your niche in this world of saints and diving in passionately.

I would be remiss if I didn't mention one of the hippest hipsters to ever hipster—G. K. Chesterton. While not a saint (yet!), he is well known to Catholic hipsters everywhere who love his writings, but most especially his famous quotation: "In Catholicism, the pint, the pipe, and the Cross can all fit together." Chesterton is considered one of the best writers of the twentieth century, penning hundreds of articles, short stories, and books. Often pictured with a monocle, a cigar, and a mustache, Chesterton is a convert to the Catholic Church, and he also assisted in C. S. Lewis's conversion to Christianity.

As much as I love to read old books, I also enjoy exploring a new take on history from authors such as Scott Hahn or Dr. Brant Pitre. These modern theologians bring to life the scriptures in new and exciting ways. Their perspectives on the history of the Mass in particular have moved me to understand this holy celebration in more ways than I could ever imagine. Learning from Dr. Pitre about the Jewish roots of the Eucharist impacted my love for the Mass significantly.

Pope Benedict XVI is a modern-day theologian who makes me marvel with everything he has to say. I first began to read his books when he was still Cardinal Ratzinger. I have great respect for Pope Benedict for a host of reasons, but one of them is his ability to really understand the world before anyone else. His understanding of the culture can be seen in his prose from the letters he wrote as pope to his Jesus of Nazareth series.

One of the greatest things about being Catholic is the abundance of writings we have access to in order to deepen our faith and our understanding of why and how we are to live in this world—tools we can use to learn and pray about our ultimate call to evangelize in the name of Jesus Christ.

I'll see you in the hidden corners of the library or at the local Barnes & Noble in the Christian theology section. I'll be the one rocking hipster glasses and clutching a cappuccino.

COOL SAINT:
ST. THOMAS AQUINAS

St. Thomas Aquinas (1225–1274) was a priest in the Dominican Order and one of the most important medieval philosophers and theologians. He is known for his prolific writings about both philosophy and theology. The works for which he is best known are the *Summa Theologica* and the *Summa Contra Gentiles*. These are both multivolume, somewhat intimidating-looking works of theology, but there are many, many single-volume compilations of Aquinas's writings that make him accessible to Catholic hipsters everywhere.

FORGOTTEN PRAYER

A Prayer before Study

Creator of all things, true source of light and wisdom, origin of all being, graciously let a ray of your light penetrate the darkness of my understanding.

Take from me the double darkness in which I have been born, an obscurity of sin and ignorance.

Give me a keen understanding, a retentive memory, and the ability to grasp things correctly and fundamentally.

Grant me the talent of being exact in my explanations and the ability to express myself with thoroughness and charm.

Point out the beginning, direct the progress, and help in the completion. I ask this through Jesus Christ our Lord. Amen.

—St. Thomas Aquinas

ACTIVITY

Start a Christian book club, and study the great books of Catholic theologians.

The best way to study theology, or the writings of saints, is to read them in community! Ask your parish if they do a small-group program, or start your own with a group of friends. Meet weekly, and whoever can come will come. Read these impressive writings, and start to unpack their power on your faith walk.

OUR LADY OF GUADALUPE

by Tommy Tighe

Growing up in Southern California, I found that Our Lady of Guadalupe's image was everywhere. She was prominently displayed at our local parish, of course, but she also made appearances at local Mexican food joints, on bumper stickers, and even as graffiti near my childhood home.

As most probably know, our Lady appeared to Juan Diego (or, as we hipsters also know him, "Cuauhtlatoatzin") back in 1531 at Tepeyac Hill near what is now Mexico City. It's a fantastic event in the history of the Catholic Church, as the miracle that followed the apparitions led to the conversion of many, and the *tilma* (Spanish for "blanket" or "cape") that bears the image of Our Lady of Guadalupe is still hanging and visible to visitors of the Guadalupe Basilica today.

The Blessed Virgin Mary has become so beloved by the Mexican people since the time of the apparition that her image is plastered from coast to coast. Sure, you've seen her on purses, T-shirts, and giant framed paintings processing down the street, but she's also been spotted hanging out in less well-known places:

- The Tailgate—One of my favorites has to be any representation of the Our Lady of Guadalupe found sprayed onto the tailgate of a Chevy Silverado driving down the Pacific Coast Highway. Not only is Mary prominently displayed but also typically an oversized face of Jesus is also displayed; often a picture of the actual truck you see driving in front of you is included to. Pure magic.

- The Tattoo—Many Catholics have a hang-up about tattoos, but as time passes, tattoos are becoming more and more mainstream. And if you're going to display something permanently on your body, why not have it be the Blessed Virgin Mary? Inking yourself up with the miraculous image depicted on the tilma is definitely a Catholic Hipster move.

- The Vestments—Sure, we know our priests love Mary, but have you ever been to a Mass where the image of the tilma was prominently displayed on the priest's vestments? That's a serious way to send a strong message to everyone at Mass that we are under the protection of her mantle and are being led by her directly to her son!

- The Coloring Pages—If you're a serious Catholic parent, chances are that you've handed your toddlers some Our Lady of Guadalupe coloring pages. Sure, they can color the same things as their non-Catholic friends, but why? Isn't it better to sit them down with a giant box of crayons to fill in the dazzling image she left for us? Yes, yes it is.

It doesn't take much to find Our Lady of Guadalupe in some pretty random places, but I think it's totally awesome and an exciting way to spread the Good News throughout the popular culture. The more we can get the image of Mary out there, the better. If we drink out of mugs, wear shirts, carry bags, and rock bumper stickers with her image, I'm certain she'll make some good come of it.

COOL SAINT: ST. MARÍA DE JESÚS SACRAMENTADO

St. María de Jesús Sacramentado is the founder of the Daughters of the Sacred Heart of Jesus. At her canonization, Pope John Paul II called her "an eloquent example of total dedication to the service of God and to suffering humanity."[9] She was well known for her selfless care of the poor and is the first canonized woman from Mexico, connecting her forever with the Mystical Rose herself.

FORGOTTEN PRAYER

A Prayer to Our Lady of Guadalupe

Our Lady of Guadalupe,
Mystical Rose,
make intercession for holy Church,
protect the sovereign pontiff,
help all those who invoke you in their necessities,
and since you are the ever Virgin Mary
and Mother of the true God,
obtain for us from your most holy Son
the grace of keeping our faith,
of sweet hope in the midst of the bitterness of life,
of burning charity, and the precious gift
of final perseverance. Amen.

ACTIVITY

If you want to come off as a hipster lover of Our Lady of Guadalupe, you're going to need to work on your pronunciation of Cuauhtlatoatzin.

You can go with "Koh-wow-tlaa-toe-OT-zeen" or "Coo-a-oo-tlaa-tot-sing" or just go with "The Talking Eagle" if the others seem too strenuous. No matter your choice, you've got to speak it with confidence.

Good luck!

AND THEN THERE IS THAT LITTLE CHAIN

by Tommy Tighe

For those looking at the Catholic Church from the outside, there are few things more Catholic than the Blessed Virgin Mary. And since our non-Catholic Christian brothers and sisters tend to find it offensive that we ask Mary to intercede on our behalf, I can barely imagine what their reaction would be if they heard about the Total Consecration to Jesus through Mary as proposed by St. Louis de Montfort!

Imagine their shock when they hear something along the lines of "perfect consecration to Jesus is but a perfect and complete consecration of oneself to the Blessed Virgin."

We Catholic hipsters know it's all true, of course. God chose the Blessed Virgin Mary to be the means by which he gave Jesus to us, and therefore, choosing the Blessed Virgin Mary as our means to give ourselves back to him makes perfect sense.

After a long and arduous thirty-three-day journey, those of us who have consecrated ourselves to Jesus through the Blessed Virgin Mary proclaim our holy slavery by means of wearing a little chain. St. Louis de Montfort describes it this way: "It is very praiseworthy and helpful for those who have become slaves of Jesus in Mary to wear, in token of their slavery of love, a little chain blessed with a special blessing."

With that instruction, countless Catholic hipsters have stopped in at their local Catholic bookstores or hopped on the Internet in search of the perfect little chain to shout their devotion to the Total Consecration from the rooftops.

Ah, but which type of chain is right? As a man, should I be in search of a huge chain that makes me look tough and masculine? As a Christian working on the virtue of humility, should I be looking for a chain so tiny that no one will ever notice? Should I go gold, silver, or nickel?

St. Louis didn't spell it out. Instead, he left it up to the Catholics who fell in love with this devotion to decide on the specifics for ourselves. But something seems right about wearing a chain as a Catholic; doesn't it?

It goes a long way to signifying that we were once chained to our sins but have broken free by our Lord's grace, and we now voluntarily chain ourselves to him through his Mother.

It's beautiful, really.

I have to admit, every time I see someone wearing an otherwise bland-looking chain around the wrist, I want to run right up, give that person a big ol' hug, and proclaim that I'm doing it all for him through her as well.

COOL SAINT:
ST. LOUIS DE MONTFORT

St. Louis de Montfort was a French priest and confessor who lived between 1673 and 1716. Other than being known as an amazing preacher who was made a missionary apostolic by Pope Clement XI, St. Louis is also recognized for writing quite a few tomes on the faith. He is best known for his devotion to the Blessed Virgin Mary as well as his practice of praying the Rosary without fail.

He developed a style of preaching that was regarded by some as strange, and this was potentially the reason for a poisoning attempt against him. While it didn't lead to his immediate demise, it is cited as the main contributing factor to his slowly deteriorating health. Louis died at the age of forty-three in April 1716, and he was canonized by Pope Pius XII in 1947.

St. Louis de Montfort, pray for us.

FORGOTTEN PRAYER

Consecration to Jesus through Mary

O Mary, Virgin most powerful and Mother of mercy, Queen of Heaven and Refuge of sinners, we consecrate ourselves to thine Immaculate Heart. We consecrate to thee our very being and our whole life; all that we have, all that we love, all that we are. To thee we give our bodies, our hearts and our souls; to thee we give our homes, our families, our country. We desire that all that is in us and around us may belong to thee, and may share in the benefits of thy motherly benediction. And that this act of consecration may be truly efficacious and lasting, we renew this day at thy feet the promises of our Baptism and our first Holy Communion. We pledge ourselves to profess courageously and at all times the truths of our holy Faith, and to live as befits Catholics who are duly submissive to all the directions of the Pope and the Bishops in communion with him. We pledge ourselves to keep the commandments of God and His Church, in particular to keep holy the Lord's Day. We likewise pledge ourselves to make the consoling practices of the Christian religion, and above all, Holy Communion, an integral part of our lives, in so far as we shall be able so to do. Finally, we promise thee, O glorious Mother of God and loving

Mother of men, to devote ourselves wholeheartedly to
the service of thy blessed cult, in order to hasten and
assure, through the sovereignty of thine Immaculate
Heart, the coming of the kingdom of the Sacred Heart
of thine adorable Son, in our own hearts and in those
of all men, in our country and in all the world, as in
heaven, so on earth. Amen.

—St. Louis de Montfort

ACTIVITY

If you want to be cool, you have to have guts!

St. Louis de Montfort refers to those who have consecrated
themselves to Jesus through Mary using his formula as slaves
of Mary. This, of course, is a slavery of love rather than a slavery of force, and it actually goes a long way toward helping
us understand how to correctly consider our position in the
order of things.

This idea of being a slave of Mary makes absolutely no
sense outside of the Catholic world. And so, if you want to be
bold with your evangelization technique, I double-dog-dare
you to bring up the fact that you are a slave of Mary during
your next conversation about faith with a non-Catholic.

Don't be afraid.

You can do it . . . and Mary will be so proud of you!

PART THREE

REDISCOVER THE LIFE

The priest at my local parish is very fond of saying that people who look at our lives should see that there is something different about us. When they look at us, they shouldn't just see another secular person going through the typical motions of daily life, but rather, they should see hope in the face of suffering, joy in the face of sorrow, and that special something they can't quite put their finger on that seems to set us apart.

Quite often, it's that thing people can't quite put their finger on that draws them into discovering or rediscovering Catholicism. This is why the best means of evangelizing for the Catholic faith is being the best darn Catholic you can be rather than reciting some magic set of words or perfect verse from scripture.

From following a calendar that sets us apart from the rest of the world, to listening to radio stations most non-Catholics don't even know exist, to offering up our pain and suffering as our grandmothers told us to, to squeezing in a quick visit to daily Mass on the way to work, the Catholic life is a beautiful expression of deep relationship with our Lord and our brothers and sisters in the faith.

The time has come for all of us to rediscover the Catholic life, because that's the only way we'll draw others back to it as well.

SEQUENCE OF SALVATION

by Matt Dunn

In accepting our cross,
We know that each gain, each loss,
Each and ev'ry thought,
Leads us through the daily grind,
Understanding what we find
May not be what we sought.

Yet, always continuing,
Moving forward while viewing
Dangers from all sides.
For in ev'ry working day,
Each weekend hike, or game we play
Temptation always hides.

So while we must bear this weight,
We know that we chose this fate,
"Accepted," as I said.
Accepted, as he had before
When we (now) know what was in store:
He'd rise from the dead.

Thus we turn our eyes to him
When our thoughts and deeds are grim
Our prayer, a whispered groan:
"I may not know what is to be,
But this cross which burdens me
Is lighter than your own."

To join with him in paradise;
Despite the tears which stained our eyes
We turn them to the east.
And see the awesome rising Son.
Knowing now what he has done:
Prepared me for the feast.

LOVING THE OLD CALENDAR

by Anna Mitchell

The Catholic hipster's proclivity for old-school Catholicism is not limited to attending the Tridentine Mass but also includes following the traditional liturgical calendar. The old calendar is not widely used in the post–Vatican II era of the Church, making a fairly exclusive club of intense Catholics who follow it.

Here are some of the features of this calendar that you will not necessarily encounter in the Novus Ordo calendar:

- Ember Days—Ember days are days of prayer and fasting that the Church set aside in each season to, according to the *Catholic Encyclopedia*, "thank God for the gifts of nature, to teach men to make use of them in moderation, and to assist the needy."[10] They take place on the Wednesday, Friday, and Saturday that follow the Feast of St. Lucy in Advent, after Ash Wednesday in Lent, after Pentecost in the spring, and after the Exaltation of the Holy Cross in the fall. The fasting formula of eating one full meal and two snack-like meals would be in effect, as well as refraining from meat.
- Rogation Days—Rogation days were set aside by the Church to pray to appease the anger of God and seek his blessings for a bountiful harvest. There is the major rogation day, which takes

place on April 25 (also the Feast of St. Mark), and three minor rogation days on the Monday, Tuesday, and Wednesday before Ascension Thursday. Rogation days are traditionally commemorated with processions and the Litany of the Saints.

- Obligatory Abstinence—There was a time in the Church when Good Friday was remembered every Friday by the faithful, who were required to abstain from meat. That practice remains for those who adhere to the old calendar. Yes, it is a small cross each week, but it also makes the celebration sweeter when a solemnity happens to land on a Friday.

- Observing Actual Feast Days—It's a common practice nowadays to move certain feasts to the nearest Sunday. The reasoning behind this is (perhaps) to ease consciences by eliminating certain Holy Days of Obligation. The Catholic hipster, of course, has no use for lazy Catholicism, and—in following the old calendar—still observes (for example) the Epiphany on January 6, the Ascension on a Thursday, and the Assumption on August 15.

- Forty Days of Christmas—On the Novus Ordo calendar, the Christmas season ends on the Feast of the Baptism of the Lord. While this certainly beats the secular world, which starts celebrating Christmas the day after Halloween and stops celebrating Christmas on December 26, following the old calendar allows you to keep your vintage Christmas decorations out until the Feast of the Presentation on February 2. That's a liturgical season worthy of celebrating the birth of the newborn King!

COOL SAINT:
BL. PIER GIORGIO FRASSATI

This guy probably wouldn't be quite so obscure in the United States if it weren't for the fact that his feast day is July 4. That being said, there is a growing devotion to him among young people, as he is the epitome of Catholic cool.

Born in 1901 in Turin, Italy, Pier Giorgio became a devoted Catholic at an early age. In his teenage years, he spent much of his time serving the poor and needy, and he later became a Catholic activist. But he wasn't one of those overly pious young Catholics who only did churchy things. He loved to climb mountains. He loved art, music, and poetry. He could quote full passages from Dante. There are photos of him with a cigar in his mouth.

He died at the age of twenty-four on July 4, 1925, after days of suffering during which he insisted that a poor man receive his medication. His body was exhumed and found incorrupt in 1981. Pope John Paul II beatified him in 1990, calling him a "Man of the Eight Beatitudes."

Bl. Pier Giorgio, pray for us.

FORGOTTEN PRAYER

The Universal Prayer

Lord, I believe in you: increase my faith.
I trust in you: strengthen my trust.
I love you: let me love you more and more.
I am sorry for my sins: deepen my sorrow.

I worship you as my first beginning,
I long for you as my last end,
I praise you as my constant helper
and call on you as my loving protector.

Guide me by your wisdom,
correct me with your justice,
comfort me with your mercy,
protect me with your power.

I offer you, Lord, my thoughts: to be fixed on you;
my words: to have you for their theme;

my actions: to reflect my love for you;
my sufferings: to be endured for your greater glory.

I want to do what you ask of me:
in the way you ask,
for as long as you ask,
because you ask it.

Lord, enlighten my understanding,
strengthen my will,
purify my heart,
and make me holy.

Help me to repent of my past sins
and to resist temptation in the future.
Help me to rise above my human weaknesses
and to grow stronger as a Christian.

Let me love you, my Lord and my God,
and see myself as I really am:
a pilgrim in this world,
a Christian called to respect and love
all whose lives I touch,
those under my authority,
my friends and my enemies.

Help me to conquer anger with gentleness,
greed by generosity,
apathy by fervor.
Help me to forget myself
and reach out toward others.

Make me prudent in planning,
courageous in taking risks.
Make me patient in suffering,
unassuming in prosperity.

Keep me, Lord, attentive at prayer,
temperate in food and drink,

diligent in my work,
firm in my good intentions.

Let my conscience be clear,
my conduct without fault,
my speech blameless,
my life well-ordered.
Put me on guard against my human weaknesses.
Let me cherish your love for me,
keep your law,
and come at last to your salvation.

Teach me to realize that this world is passing,
that my true future is the happiness of heaven,
that life on earth is short,
and the life to come eternal.

Help me to prepare for death
with a proper fear of judgment,
but a greater trust in your goodness.
Lead me safely through death
to the endless joy of heaven.

Grant this through Christ our Lord. Amen.

—Pope Clement XI

ACTIVITY

Make a point to observe the feast days on the actual day they were meant to be observed. This may involve going to a normal daily Mass if your parish follows the practice of moving these feasts to the nearest Sunday, but if you have a traditional parish nearby, chances are there are several Holy Day Masses that you can attend at your convenience.

Bonus activity: Don't put up your Christmas decorations until a day or two before Christmas, and leave them up until

February 2. (You might need to water your tree a few times to keep it from shedding its needles all over the place!)

CATHOLIC RADIO

by Tommy Tighe

There are many people who have no idea that it even exists, and yet there it is, blasting out the truth of the Catholic faith twenty-four hours a day, seven days a week, 365 days a year: Catholic radio.

You might try and tell me that radio is a thing of the past, and to a certain extent you may be right, but Catholic radio is fighting against the tide and keeping up with the ever-changing landscape of media and communication.

To be honest, I went quite a while without knowing that Catholic radio existed. I owe my discovery to the fact that I experienced a transition at work that led to a lot of downtime. Don't ask me why, but I took out my smartphone (a Palm Pre at the time, if anyone remembers that piece of junk), clicked on a very archaic Tune In Radio app, and searched for "Catholic."

That moment, motivated by God knows what (most likely because it was motivated by God himself), is the exact moment to which I can trace my reversion back to the faith. Up until then, I was a cradle Catholic who had been going through the motions for the majority of my life. Sure, I continued going to Mass each and every Sunday throughout my wild ride at UC Santa Barbara, but I wasn't really engaging in the faith, and

I definitely wasn't embracing all the things that the Catholic Church was trying to tell me were true.

Catholic radio changed all that. I stumbled very quickly upon two shows that changed my life, as I'm sure they have done for countless others: EWTN's *Open Line* and *Catholic Answers Live*. These two radio shows, completely simplistic and ordinary in format, became my gateway back into the full banquet of the Church. The questions I had always had were being answered each and every day, and after a short time, *I* knew the answers, knew the persuasive arguments, and even knew the chapters and verses to back it all up.

Imagine that! A cradle Catholic who knew a thing or two about the faith, and I owe it all to the jump start that Catholic radio gave me.

All these years later, it remains the only thing blasting from the speakers during my morning and afternoon commutes (unless, of course, I'm in need of some straight up '90s hip hop . . . you can't deny that urge), and all these years later it remains a source of truth, comfort, and guidance in my spiritual journey.

Hop in your car, flip on Catholic radio, and enjoy.

COOL SAINT:
ST. MAXIMILIAN KOLBE

The great St. Maximilian Kolbe's heroic example of putting others before himself in the most profound way during the Second World War is the stuff of legends. Also, he had a pretty remarkable beard that most Catholic hipsters look to for inspiration during "No Shave November."

But not many know about St. Max's radio career. When he returned home to Poland in 1938 following a myriad of missionary trips that resulted in winning countless souls for Christ, he founded a radio station known as Radio Niepokalanów.

He maintained his amateur radio license with the call sign "SP3RN."

His selfless example at Auschwitz as Prisoner #16670 in 1941 was the icing on the cake for this unbelievably heroic modern-day saint.

St. Maximilian Kolbe, pray for us.

FORGOTTEN PRAYER

Prayer for Catholic Radio

God our Father, we humbly seek your all-powerful blessing on the work we have begun and ask you to bring it to completion. Give success to the work of our hands.

Lord Jesus, we seek your blessing on this radio station and ask you to consecrate it to the bold proclamation of your living Word, proclaimed in the midst of your one, holy, catholic, and apostolic Church. Guard us from the evil one and from all those who would sow destruction or despair. Keep us in communion of mind and heart with our pope and bishops, upon whom we invoke your mercy.

Spirit of God, rain upon our labors your sevenfold gifts that we may make known in truth and love the voice of Jesus. Keep us ever faithful to your inspirations, always open to the Truth, and never allow us to be conquered by pride. Create unity in our work, and broadcast through us the seeds of the Word. Make us instruments of reconciliation among all your people, and of genuine renewal and reform.

Mother of the Word Incarnate, remember this work as you come into the presence of your Son. Help us to remain humble in the image of your own heart, and guide us to the Heart of your Son. Protect us from all evil, and bring to us the God of Life whom you bore in your womb and nursed at your breast. Help us to proclaim the greatness of the Lord and to ever rejoice in God our Savior. May the offering of our service and the prayer of the blessed Archangel Gabriel, patron of radio broadcasting, be acceptable in your sight, O Lord.

Lord, show us your mercy and love and grant us your salvation. Glory be to the Father and to the Son and to the Holy Spirit, as it was in the beginning, is now, and ever shall be world without end. Amen.[11]

ACTIVITY

Do you have a woefully long commute to and from work as I do? If so, I have a remedy for the excruciating repetition of the same ten songs played over and over again on popular FM radio stations: take the forty-day Catholic Radio Challenge!

Find your local Catholic radio station (trust me, it's there, and you just don't know it), and listen on your commute to and from work for forty days.

OFFERING IT UP

by Anna Mitchell

One of the telltale signs of a true Catholic hipster is enjoyment of suffering. That is why every hipster should be Catholic, because the Catholic Church is the one place where suffering is not only an acceptable means of holiness, it's actually the highest form of holiness—when offered up.

"Offer it up." It's a phrase that Catholic children may have heard from their parents but more likely from their grandparents, who lived at a time when sacrificial living was more in vogue—or at least less avoidable. Nowadays, in a world full of drugs, credit cards, and on-demand video, the idea of sacrifice and suffering is sacrilege. But the fact of the matter is that we have the opportunity to use our sufferings (whether we choose them or not) in God's plan of salvation. It's not just an opportunity, though. It's an imperative.

Let's back up. As Christians, we are called to imitate Christ. What did Christ do? He suffered. He endured one of the most painful forms of death known to the world in order to take upon himself the wages of sin, offering his body so that, through the Resurrection, salvation could be ours. While everything Christ did and said in the three years leading up to the Crucifixion is certainly important, none of it would matter without his Passion, Death, and subsequent Resurrection.

We hear a lot of people happily spout the idea of seeing the world through Jesus' eyes. Well, just remember that you have to be nailed to the cross in order to see anything through Jesus' eyes. Let's face it: he's God, and he could have chosen to bring about the salvation of the world by any method. Being the original and ultimate hipster that he is, he chose to suffer.

While we don't necessarily have to *choose* to suffer, we do have the choice to unite our sufferings to the suffering of Jesus on the Cross, thereby participating in the redemption of the world. While there is certainly nothing lacking in the sufferings of Christ to the point that he'd somehow need our help in this regard, he does give us the opportunity to join him. How do we do that? By "offering it up."

"Offer it up" is really an incomplete phrase. Offer it up for what? For the poor souls in purgatory, for the spiritual or physical healing of a sick friend, for those living in poverty, for peace, for the holiness of a family member, for your own holiness, for whatever person in the world needs it most at that moment—for any number of intentions.

So how does one actually go about offering it up? You simply say so in prayer. Half the battle is merely remembering in the midst of your suffering, whether big or small, that God can actually use it for some good. Then you just tell him to do so.

Some hipsters may think it's cool to suffer just for the sake of suffering. But it's actually way more hip to use our daily suffering for a higher purpose.

COOL SAINT:
BL. CHIARA LUCE BADANO

Chiara Badano (nicknamed *Luce*—Italian for "light"—by the founder of the Focolare Movement) was no stranger to suffering in her short life. In fact, she welcomed it.

Born in 1979 in Sasello, Italy, Chiara grew up a normal kid. She was diagnosed at seventeen with osteosarcoma, a very painful form of cancer. Where most teenagers might have fallen into despair when faced with such a diagnosis, Chiara used her sickness as an opportunity to grow closer to the Lord and serve the people around her. Her friends and family recount the great love that she projected in the midst of suffering through her cancer treatments. They report that, despite the incredible pain, she even refused morphine, complaining that it would take away her lucidity. She said, "I can only offer my pain to Jesus. It's all I have left."

Chiara Luce Badano died on October 7, 1990, just shy of her nineteenth birthday. She was beatified twenty years later in 2010.

Bl. Chiara Luce Badano, pray for us.

FORGOTTEN PRAYER

Invocations to the Sacred Heart of Jesus

Heart of Jesus, who has borne all our griefs, strengthen me.

Heart of Jesus, who has weighed this sorrow before sending it to us, help me.

Heart of Jesus, ever touched by the sight of sorrows, pity me.

Heart of Jesus, beautiful in thy sorrows, teach me to become holy by means of this affliction.

Heart of Jesus, spending thyself for souls in the midst of thy sorrows, make me unselfish in bearing mine.

Heart of Jesus, troubled at the grave of Lazarus, comfort those who mourn.

Heart of Jesus, softened by the tears of Magdalen, pity the sorrowful.

Heart of Jesus, whose sorrow was ever before thee,
    teach us to unite our griefs to thine.
Heart of Jesus, agonized in Gethsemane, strengthen us
    in all the sorrows of life.
Heart of Jesus, whose unknown agonies we shall know
    and love in heaven, teach us to suffer alone with
    God for his glory.
Heart of Jesus, broken with love and sorrow on the
    Cross, draw us to thyself in our sorrows, and make
    us faithful in them to the end. Amen.

ACTIVITY

Come up with a minor mortification to practice on a daily basis. Many holy people have worn hair shirts or even practiced self-flagellation, but it's not wise to do such things without proper spiritual direction. You could instead wear a small woolen scapular, put a pebble in your shoe, resolve always to take the stairs, or refrain from meat every Friday instead of just during Lent. Being able to deny yourself with small crosses helps you learn to renounce yourself when the big crosses come along, should you be so chosen.

REDISCOVER BLOGS

by Lisa M. Hendey

While I'm not quite a cord cutter officially (yet), it's rare that I turn on a television these days. I've found that when breaking news hits, I'm more likely to turn to Twitter than to mainstream media for instantaneous information. There is something about having the firsthand perspective of those on the ground that is both fresh and a call for prayer.

A recent example of this occurred in April 2015 when a 7.8 magnitude earthquake struck Nepal, killing nearly 9,000 people. I found myself immediately turning to Twitter for reports on the devastation. But I also turned quickly to trusted blogging sources who could report not only on the details of the calamity but also on ways in which our families could support the nearly half-a-million souls in need of immediate support.

Even in the day-to-day news cycle, I find myself more likely to turn to blogs than to traditional news sources. Even in an age when social media usage is eclipsing blog traffic, blogs—and especially Catholic blogs—afford the opportunity to learn, to discover, and to discuss the news from a uniquely Catholic perspective. I often find when reading blog posts that some of the best information is contained in the comment boxes, where invested readers often expand upon the perspective of the author.

However, *Caveat emptor* is a good motto when plunging into the blogosphere, even if the content is free (if you don't count sidebar advertising). Most bloggers are not trained journalists, so readers must consider accuracy standards and ethical considerations to be different from what you'd find coming out of the corporate newsrooms. And those same comboxes that can yield amazing pearls of wisdom can also become minefields of outright hatred. Bring up politics, the president, homeschooling, Mass preferences, or even sometimes pro-life philosophies, and you might want to be prepared for debate.

So why bother? In an age when journalism continues to be an ever-morphing concept, why should we even try to keep up with what's happening in the world around us?

We Catholics are called to be in the world but not of it. To live in line with Catholic social teaching we must be men and women who are tuned in and turned on. It's not enough simply to read the news. As people of faith and followers of Christ, we are called beyond watching and into witnessing. When we see a need happening around us, we must follow the teachings of Christ, who told us to emulate the model of the Good Samaritan. Being a Catholic news junkie these days means not only staying on top of the headlines but also prayerfully considering how we can be consistent in our faithful citizenship and our solidarity with those in need.

COOL SAINT:
VEN. FULTON J. SHEEN

Ven. Fulton J. Sheen definitely would have been a Catholic blogger had he lived in our time. Sheen would have tweeted. His YouTube videos would have gone viral. He probably would have even livestreamed from the New York subway.

A son of the twentieth century, Archbishop Sheen—whose cause for canonization is currently in transition—pivoted from founder of a successful radio show to host of the wildly popular television program *Life Is Worth Living*. More than thirty million viewers tuned in weekly to hear the two-time Emmy Award–winning bishop discuss the news and moral issues of his day. In an age when likes or retweets can determine the algorithm and create "news," we would do well to pray through the intercession of Ven. Fulton Sheen, who once said, "The proud man counts his newspaper clippings, the humble man his blessings."

FORGOTTEN PRAYER

I keep a small statue of St. Michael the Archangel next to my computer workstation. It feels fitting to invoke the intercession of this warrior angel against the evil that is often so pervasive in today's world.

> St. Michael the Archangel, defend us in battle. Be our defense against the wickedness and snares of the devil. May God rebuke him, we humbly pray. And you, O Prince of the heavenly host, by the power of God, thrust into hell Satan and all the other evil spirits who prowl the world for the ruin of souls. Amen.

ACTIVITY

This week, make an effort to discover, read, and share one new Catholic blog. Get outside your comfort zone by leaving at least one charitable comment for the blogger. Or better yet, write an actual e-mail to the blog's editor and let him or her know what you enjoyed about the blog and how your visit could be enhanced in the future. Most bloggers are unpaid writers who share their gifts as a means of sharing the Good News. Up the ante on the tone of digital dialogue by engaging in at least one positive digital conversation in the Catholic blogosphere this week.

COOL CATHOLIC BABY NAMES

by Katherine Morna Towne

American baby naming has undergone a major shift in recent years. Name expert Laura Wattenberg (author of the book *The Baby Name Wizard* and its associated website) describes this shift: "There is a revolution going on when it comes to baby names, and for some parents, the more unusual, the better. . . . Past generations worried more about their child fitting in, but today's parents want their kids to stand out. And some are in a race to be more distinctive than the next."[12]

In her 1999 name book *Puffy, Xena, Quentin, Uma*, author Joal Ryan referenced this revolution when she described parents who "troll underwater caves to find the *perfect* name" as "spelunkers,"[13] which was just brilliant—parents today *are* naming spelunkers, and Catholic parents are just as susceptible as any others. But instead of spelunking, we Catholics go *catacombing*. Yes, we do. Down into the hallowed candlelit crypts of the Church of the ancient and near past we go, looking for new/old names that might perfectly suit our little Catholic babies.

Perhaps, like so many other parents of today, we do want our kids to stand out through their names. But I argue that our motivations are less driven by the common modern hope that our offspring will be seen as unique and special and more driven by a desire to evangelize and catechize, to baptize the world and set it on fire, even through the oft-hidden life of baby bearing and child raising. We follow our beloved St. John Paul II and joyfully sing our Easter Alleluia any way we can.[14] I have always loved the names of our faith and have had the great privilege of being invited into the baby-name conversations of many, many faith-filled couples via name consultations I offer through my blog. I've delighted in seeing the range of taste in names chosen by the couples I consider to be the name-catacombing kind. In my experience, these can be broken into three groups.

I'M CATHOLIC AND YOU KNOW IT

These parents choose names that are obviously Catholic to the rest of the world. For example, most people, I think, would know who a little John Paul was likely named after (because non-Catholics—or non-fans of JPII, Catholic or otherwise—would not likely put themselves in the position of having to say, every time, "No! He's *not* named for the pope!" Right?). A little Maria Regina (double first name, thank you very much) would still be called out as Catholic, I think. Xavier's losing some of its Catholic-only cachet as it rises in popularity, but even still, I think most people are familiar enough with St. Francis Xavier to make the connection.

I KNOW THE SECRET PAPAL PASSWORD(S)

I'm not saying that these kinds of parents think of themselves as belonging to an exclusive club—the Church is for everyone, after all; come on in!—but upon hearing of the birth of a little Zelie or Gianna, only a Catholic of the papist variety is likely to immediately recognize the reference to our new St. Zélie Martin and her sister in heaven, St. Gianna Beretta Molla. Or how about Karoline? Not everyone knows that St. John

Paul II's birth name was Karol, but there's a good chance your Mass-loving, Rosary-saying, NFP practicing Catholic friend knows. And St. Joachim! His name seems more likely to be recognized in America as an alternate spelling of NBA player Joakim Noah's name than that of our Lady's papa—except to those who keep up with the Church calendar and her feast days.

I LOVE ~~WEIRD~~ UNUSUAL NAMES, AND THE CHURCH IS A GOLDMINE

Catholic or not, parents of the unusual-names persuasion like to find names that no one's heard of—the rarer the better. The Catholic unusual-names parents feel it's important to stick to names related to our faith and delight in that requirement. Their list may include names such as Jurmin and Jarlath, Daudi and Dafrosa, Soprata and Soteris—all of whom are bona fide saints. Or they might light up at nouns-as-names, such as Vesper, Tiber, Caeli, and Rosary (I know of little ones with each of those names). It's possible that no one they know or meet, whether at church or not, will know anything about the names they chose (well, except Rosary), but in educating those who ask, they are evangelizing in a unique way and are excited to do so. (Names are actually a great tool of the New Evangelization—how often would you normally have the chance to tell others about the heroes of our faith, the lovers of our Lord, in a lighthearted, engaging, and even fun way?)

St. John Chrysostom said, "So let the name of the saints enter our homes through the naming of our children, to train not only the child but the father, when he reflects that he is the father of John or Elijah or James. . . . Do not because it is a small thing regard it as small; its purpose is to succor us." Canon 855 in the Code of Canon Law states that "parents, sponsors, and the pastor are to take care that a name foreign to Christian sensibility is not given." Mother Church has given us beautiful, protective, and freeing guidelines to follow when naming our beloved babies, and Catholic hipsters use this freedom to witness to and draw strength from our faith even in the very names we yell out on the playground. And yes, I would totally consider Chrysostom and Canon to be legit possibilities for a Catholic baby.

COOL SAINT: ST. JOACHIM

St. Joachim is the father of our Lady, husband of St. Anne. Though he's not mentioned in scripture, the Church has long revered him as a saint. He's the patron of fathers, grandfathers, grandparents, married couples, cabinetmakers, and linen traders; he shares his feast day of July 26 with St. Anne.

His obscurity in the United States is, in my opinion, a direct result of his name. The English pronunciation "JO-ah-kim" is unfamiliar and counterintuitive for a lot of Americans, and the pronunciations used in the parts of the world where the name is more familiar are very different from the English pronunciation. Add in the variant that's most familiar to Americans—the Spanish Joaquín, pronounced "hwah-KEEN"—and the common assumption becomes that Joachim is said "hwah-KEEM". Or perhaps "HO-kum". Or is the "ch" pronounced as a "ch" rather than a "k"? And why would anyone want to name a baby after an NBA player or a Hollywood actor anyway? Argh!

St. Joachim deserves better! Tradition holds that he and St. Anne suffered from infertility, and they prayed for a baby. Their daughter, the Blessed Virgin Mary, Mother of the Messiah, was a blessing given to them in their old age; their grandson is Jesus Christ himself. St. Joachim is a powerful patron for any little boy to have and a powerful intercessor for us all.

St. Joachim, pray for us.

FORGOTTEN PRAYER

Oh my dear Mother Mary! Oh my beloved Jesus! May your most sweet Names always live in my own and in all hearts. May I forget all other names, that I may remember and always invoke no one but your adored Names. Ah Jesus, my Redeemer! And my Mother Mary, when the moment of my death shall arrive, and my soul shall depart from this life, by your merits grant me the grace then to utter my last accents, repeating: I love you, Jesus and Mary; Jesus and Mary, I give you my heart and my soul. Amen.

—St. Alphonsus Liguori

ACTIVITY

Quiz: What Kind of Catholic Namer Am I?

(1) You feel it's important to give your daughter a Marian name. Which are you most likely to choose?
  a) Mary
  b) Regina
  c) Carmel
  d) Monserrat

(2) You think giving your son a Marian name is:
  a) not really something you're comfortable with
  b) cool if it counts to use a male name connected to her (such as Joseph)
  c) awesome, because you love that so many male saints have Mary/Marie/Maria as a middle name
  d) awesome! You totally think Theotokos could work as a first name

(3) You want to give your baby a papal name. Which would you be most likely to choose?
   a)   John
   b)   John Paul
   c)   Linus
   d)   Lando

(4) You like going off-road to find other names connected to saints—their birth names or nicknames or last names, or maybe the name of the places they were born or died. Which of these are you most drawn to?
   a)   You don't go off-road with saints' names
   b)   Baptiste, for St. John the Baptist
   c)   Bosco, for St. John Bosco
   d)   Euphrosyne, Greek for "joy" and St. Catherine of Siena's childhood nickname

(5) You heard a mom calling out to her son "Nash" on the playground and discover in the course of conversation that his given name is Athanasius. You think this is:
   a)   confusing—why not a name like Peter or Paul?
   b)   creative, but not your style
   c)   pretty darn great, and you add it to your own running list for future children
   d)   a little too tame—it's the full Athanasius all the time or nothing at all

If you answered with

. . . mostly a's: *Familiar Namer*
Congratulations! You are a familiar namer—you like the solid safety of names such as Margaret, Charles, and Clare and think they do a fine job of representing the faith. Based on this alone, you likely wouldn't qualify as a name-catacombing Catholic hipster, and you're likely more than fine with that.

. . . mostly b's: *I'm Catholic and You Know It*
Congratulations! You like names that let others know you love
your faith, as long as they're not too out there. You'll consider a
double name such as John Paul or Mary Clare, and you prefer
Thérèse to the other Teresa variants because it's more obviously
saintly, but you'll leave Gemma and Jogues to someone more
adventurous.

. . . mostly c's: *I Know the Secret Papal Password(s)*
Congratulations! You're the kind of namer who likes to dig
deep to find new ideas for faith-filled names. You might name
your daughter Sabeth after St. Elizabeth of the Trinity's childhood nickname or Zoe after St. Catherine of Laboure's birth
name. You might name a boy Becket after St. Thomas Becket
or Bennett knowing that it's a form of Benedict. There isn't
too much that's off limits as long as it can be traced back to
the faith.

. . . mostly d's: *I Love ~~Weird~~ Unusual Names, and the Church
Is a Goldmine*
Congratulations! You are a bold and fearless namer, one who
seeks out the cobwebbiest corners of the world of Catholic
names and gets excited at the need for asterisked explanations
after your name picks. Because of you, long-forgotten saints
have a chance of making their way back into Catholic con-
sciousness and having their intercession invoked. Thank you!

AH! CONFESSION

by Tiffany Walsh

I remember my first trip to the confessional very well. I was eight years old, and my entire religious-education class was receiving the sacrament for the first time. First Communion, coming down the pike a few months hence, I was excited about, but the sacrament of Reconciliation (commonly referred to simply as Confession)? Not so much.

I was nervous about going into that confessional and admitting to making poor choices, and the fact of the matter is that not much has changed in the intervening years. For a time as a young adult, I even convinced myself that going to Confession was not necessary and that I did not need to worry about it anymore. Although my feelings about the sacrament have changed to become much more positive, I indeed still feel anxiety about going.

This is the way journeys to Confession usually unfold for me. There is only one time slot per week offered at my parish, and it is rarely opportune for me to attend. Therefore, I seek out other parishes throughout the week, and frequently, although my intentions are always good, I miss those time slots too. I convince myself that I need to stop off at the grocery store to pick something up for dinner or that I am very tired from being up with a sick child overnight and should just try again next week. Deep down, I still dread making myself so vulnerable in front of another person.

Inevitably, several weeks go by before I actually set foot in a church with the goal of going to Confession. By then, I am feeling guilty that I let so much time elapse and am more anxious than ever about the whole situation. All of this, of course, is completely self-inflicted.

Recently, I went through the above-mentioned avoidance acrobatics and finally, three weeks later, pulled up to the parish that is associated with my son's school. There is a Tuesday afternoon slot for Confession there, and I stopped on my way home from work. I performed an examination of conscience out in my car using the Confession app and then bravely headed to the side door of the church. I pulled on it, and nothing happened. It was locked.

I spent an awkward minute cupping my hands around my eyes to peer inside the glass but could not spy anybody inside. I thought for a fleeting moment, with relief, about leaving and trying again the next week, but my conscience pricked me to try the front door. So I did. It was also locked.

I turned around and saw an older woman walking across the street toward the church, her gait slowed by an obvious ailment in her leg. Although she could have been walking to another location down the street, I had a sense that she too was heading to Confession. I waited, and sure enough, she walked up to the front door and tried to open it. Now we were both stranded outside, looking in.

She remarked that it was very odd for the church to be locked when Confession was scheduled and encouraged me to come along with her to the other side of the church, where there is an entrance connected to the school and rectory. I followed her, but by this point I was *really* itching to head back to my car, figuring we were on a wild-goose chase.

When we got to that door, my appointed guardian angel knocked loudly, and to my surprise, a woman came and opened it! It was someone who worked at the parish, and she said that Father must have accidentally forgotten to open the outer church doors prior to heading into the confessional.

We thanked her, and while my new friend stopped off to chat for a moment, I headed into the church and to the confessional. As I was praying afterward, I reflected on how God works in our lives if we are open to hearing his voice in small but important ways. I gave just the slightest willingness to take more time in seeking out Confession, and God provided a way for me to receive the sacramental graces this encounter provides. As ever, while in the confessional receiving absolution, and immediately afterward as I prayed, I felt the soothing balm of healing and forgiveness that this sacrament brings.

As I stood to leave the church, I saw my friend in line beside the confessional, and she waved to me enthusiastically. I waved back and thought of how much God loves to bring simple comforts into our lives. Confession does not have to be intimidating—it is an opportunity for God to show us how much he loves us, always.

COOL SAINT:
ST. JOHN VIANNEY

St. John Vianney was born in 1786 near Lyon, France, into a devout Catholic family. His childhood during the French Revolution found the family risking their lives to attend Mass in secret. St. John looked up to the heroic priests who put their lives on the line to administer the sacraments.

As a young adult, St. John studied for the priesthood and was ordained in 1815. Three years later, he was sent to minister in a remote town in northern France. Now known as the Curé of Ars, he earned a legendary reputation as a confessor that remains to this day.

He loved to make himself available in the confessional, and he heard confessions for up to sixteen hours per day. As knowledge about his commitment to—and spiritual insight within—the confessional grew, so did the numbers of people who sought him out as a confessor. Penitents came from many miles away to have St. John hear their confessions. St. John also practiced daily mortifications throughout his life, denying himself food and sleep, all toward keeping himself firmly focused on his duties as a priest. He died in 1859 at age seventy-three.

John Vianney was beatified in 1905 and canonized in 1925. His feast day is August 4, and he is the patron of priests.

St. John Vianney, pray for us.

FORGOTTEN PRAYER

O my God, help me to make a good Confession. Mary, my dearest Mother, pray to Jesus for me. Help me to examine my conscience, enable me to obtain true sorrow for my sins, and beg for me the grace rather to die than to offend God again. Lord Jesus, light of our souls, who enlightens every man coming into this world, enlighten my conscience and my heart by Thy Holy Spirit, so that I may perceive all that is displeasing to Thy divine majesty and may expiate it by humble confession, true contrition, and sincere repentance.

—St. Alphonsus Liguori

ACTIVITY

Here are five simple methods of preparing for Confession for anxious souls:

- Pray—An ideal prayer prior to Confession is an examination of conscience that proceeds through each of the Ten

Commandments. As we pray we identify the sins that we have committed against each commandment. I do not know about you, but I am a person who finds lists very calming when I am nervous or overwhelmed. Sometimes I even make notes of the things I want to mention, or I keep track of them in my Confession app.

- Love—Remind yourself that God loves you and is happy that you are seeking out the sacrament, regardless of the type and number of sins you have to confess.
- Grace—Sacraments infuse grace, and Confession is no exception. We may not see a change, but we will feel one!
- Solidarity—Above, I mentioned my anxiety at making myself vulnerable in front of another person while at Confession. It now helps me to remember that I am not alone in this. We are all in this together! Even priests avail themselves of the sacrament of Reconciliation, and then they are creating that vulnerability in front of a brother priest. Humbling? Most certainly!
- Peace—The peace that transcends all understanding is available to us in the sacraments. God knows that we are not perfect and invites us simply to try again. We only have to garner the courage to accept his invitation.

THE EXTRAORDINARY FORM OF THE MASS

by Anna Mitchell

A true Catholic hipster is not capable of tolerating bad liturgy, and so it stands to reason that you would not find him or her taking any chances, if possible, when it comes to Sunday Mass. That is why you will usually find the Catholic hipster at the Extraordinary Form, also known as the Traditional Latin Mass, also known as the Tridentine Mass—the ultimate in old-school Catholic traditions.

There are a number of reasons why the Extraordinary Form is truly the hipster form of the Mass.

First, you will encounter the true beauty of the Holy Sacrifice of the Mass, especially when it comes to music (a major issue for the hipster class). Walk into any given parish on a Sunday morning, and if you're lucky, there will be a choir that sings in the same key as the organ. But there's a good chance that you'll be hearing the Mass in the musical stylings preferred by whoever is leading the music that hour—and so you could be attending the Hippie Sing-Along Mass, the Disney Princess Mass, the Jazz Mass, or the Rock Band Mass, just to name a few. When you walk into a Traditional Latin Mass, however, you are assured of sacred polyphony, chant, or silence—or a combination of them. While it may not be the style of music you collect on vinyl, it is at least a style that actually fits with what's happening on the altar.

Second, there is no possibility for silliness on the altar. Priests who take the time to learn and celebrate the Mass in the Extraordinary Form do not stray from the rubrics, if only because it's incredibly difficult to ad-lib in Latin.

Third, there is not much in the way of participation on the part of the congregation. Upon first glance, this may not seem to be an advantage over the Novus Ordo (or "New Mass"), which demands quite a bit of congregational participation. Hipsters never feel the need to be part of a crowd, and so a Mass that requires little more than the occasional *"et cum spirito tuo"* is the perfect setting for them to be alone with God while still maintaining the community aspect inherent in Catholicism. Plus, the Catholic hipster knows that the Mass is not ultimately dependent on the presence of any one person in the congregation, and so there is no need for participation trophies in his or her spiritual life.

Fourth, the Mass is celebrated with the priest's back to the people. This is also known, more properly of course, as *ad orientem* worship. This is the preferable orientation for the Catholic hipster because a priest who faces the people is a priest whose back is to Jesus in the tabernacle. And so, rather than creating a sort of Kumbaya circle in the church, the entire congregation—led by the priest—is facing liturgical east, which is the way it was always meant to be.

These are just a few of the many reasons that the Catholic hipster's preferred liturgy is the Traditional Latin Mass. This is the style of worship that will truly elevate a hipster's soul to the Lord and allow him or her to enter into the sacred mysteries.

COOL SAINT: ST. PIUS X

Cardinal Guiseppe Sarto had the unfortunate luck of being elected pope after the great Pope Leo XIII, of *Rerum Novarum* fame. Cardinal Sarto, then the patriarch of Venice, was elected supreme pontiff in 1903. Though he didn't consider himself worthy of the job, he did accept his election and took the name Pius X. And he certainly took his position seriously. During his time as pope, he lowered the age for First Holy Communion, encouraged frequent and even daily reception of the Blessed Sacrament, promoted Bible reading among the faithful, and reformed the liturgy—particularly when it came to music, bringing back Gregorian chant to the Mass. And being a lover of vintage (read: traditional) Catholicism, he was a true warrior against modernism—earning the "Hipster Pope" title because, as one meme reads, he "opposed relativism before it was cool."

As he wrote in his encyclical letter *Notre Charge Apostolique,* "Indeed, the true friends of the people are neither revolutionaries, nor innovators: they are traditionalists."

St. Pius X, pray for us.

FORGOTTEN PRAYER

The Divine Praises

Blessed be God.
Blessed be his Holy Name.
Blessed be Jesus Christ, true God and true man.
Blessed be the Name of Jesus.
Blessed be his Most Sacred Heart.
Blessed be his Most Precious Blood.
Blessed be Jesus in the Most Holy Sacrament of the
    Altar.
Blessed be the Holy Spirit, the Paraclete.
Blessed be the great Mother of God, Mary most holy.
Blessed be her holy and Immaculate Conception.

Blessed be her glorious Assumption.
Blessed be the name of Mary, Virgin and Mother.
Blessed be St. Joseph, her most chaste spouse.
Blessed be God in his angels and in his saints.

ACTIVITY

Challenge: Memorize the *Pater Noster* (aka, the Our Father in Latin). Once you've got that down, memorize the other congregation parts in the Tridentine Mass.

FINDING MARY IN THE BIBLE

by Tommy Tighe

Where is *that* in the Bible? It's a question many Catholics hear and then immediately feel an urge to start running for the door. We believe and hold certain truths that are not spelled out in the Bible explicitly enough for some of our non-Catholic brothers and sisters, and while we believe them with all our hearts, we shrink back in fear when asked to show *why* we believe them.

Luckily for us, there isn't anything in the Bible that says everything we believe has to be in the Bible! That being said, typical Catholic hipsters love them some Bible *and* love them some Blessed Virgin Mary. And as we all know, if there is any Catholic teaching that gets attacked for being "unbiblical," it's our teaching on Mary.

We believe Mary is the Mother of God; we believe she was immaculately conceived and did not sin throughout her life; we believe she was perpetually a virgin (before, during, and after the birth of Jesus); and we even believe she was assumed body and soul into heaven.

Those claims get some pretty serious looks of skepticism from our non-Catholic buddies (and we haven't even mentioned the ideas of Mary as co-redemptrix and mediatrix . . . don't even get me started). But, in reality, Catholics are the only ones taking a look at the Bible *in its entirety* and believing *everything* that's there, most especially when it comes to the crown of creation, our Lady.

And so, my dearest Catholic hipsters, don't be afraid to present your friends with a nice little biblical rundown of Mary and the implications of what the Bible says about her:

- Genesis 3:15—Way back in the beginning, we get a pretty clear reference to Mary, and it may be the moment in scripture that most clearly points to her Immaculate Conception. God says, "I will put enmity between you and the woman, and between your offspring and hers."
- Isaiah 7:14—The prophet lays out that a virgin will be the one to bring the Messiah our way when he says, "The young woman, pregnant and about to bear a son, shall name him Emmanuel."
- Luke 1:28—The Annunciation is the moment when Mary agrees to the plans of God and when God gives us a little glimpse into the Church's understanding that Mary remained sinless throughout her life, as we hear the angel Gabriel say, "Hail, favored one! The Lord is with you."
- Luke 1:39–45—The Visitation shows us a great interaction between Mary and her cousin that underscores the seemingly obvious teaching that Mary is the Mother of God, as Elizabeth states, "And how does this happen to me, that the mother of my Lord should come to me?"
- Luke 2:7—The Nativity of Jesus is that epic moment when God took on human flesh and came to us through the Blessed Virgin Mary.
- Luke 2:41–51—With the finding of the Child Jesus in the Temple, Mary shows us that she's a real mother with authentic feelings and teaches us how to ponder things in our hearts.
- John 2:1–5—It is the wedding feast at Cana at which Mary clearly shows her intercessory power and desire to bring our needs to her son, who takes this opportunity to let us know that she is

"the woman" spoken of way back in Genesis, and where she gives us one of the most important commands found in scripture: "Do whatever he tells you."

- John 19:26–27—The Crucifixion is where Jesus uses his last breath to remind us that Mary is "the woman" and to give his Mother to us and us to her.
- Acts 2:1–4—Pentecost finds Mary hanging out with the apostles during their most difficult time and at the moment when the Holy Spirit descends upon them.
- Revelation 11:19—The vision of St. John clearly shows us that Mary is the Ark of the Covenant, something that blew my mind during my reversion and still does to this very day.

You no longer need to fear the occasions when you are called to explain your love and devotion to Mary from the Bible. Everything we teach about her is right there for everyone to see, and she's waiting for everyone to realize it, turn to her, and hold her hand as she leads us home to her Son.

COOL SAINT:
ST. IRENAEUS OF LYONS

St. Irenaeus is perhaps the earliest of the Church Fathers to develop a thorough Mariology. He had a firm understanding of Mary's role in salvation history and was one of the first to speak of the connection between Eve and Mary. His writings influenced St. Ambrose and Tertullian, who both went even further in their development and understanding of Mariology.

St. Irenaeus of Lyons, pray for us!

FORGOTTEN PRAYER

The Magnificat

My soul proclaims the greatness of the Lord;
    my spirit rejoices in God my savior.
For he has looked upon his handmaid's lowliness;

behold, from now on will all ages call me blessed.
The Mighty One has done great things for me,
  and holy is his name.
His mercy is from age to age
  to those who fear him.
He has shown might with his arm,
  dispersed the arrogant of mind and heart.
He has thrown down the rulers from their thrones
  but lifted up the lowly.
The hungry he has filled with good things;
  the rich he has sent away empty.
He has helped Israel his servant
  remembering his mercy,
according to his promise to our fathers,
  to Abraham and to his descendants forever.
  (Lk 1:46–55)
Glory to the Father and to the Son and to the Holy
  Spirit,
as it was in the beginning, is now, and will be forever.
  Amen.

ACTIVITY

The Hail Mary.

It's a prayer that we learned very early on in our walk with the Catholic faith. At some point, it easily became something we rattle off from memory with little to no thought put into the powerful words we are actually saying.

Fortunately, the amazing and talented Sarah Reinhard has a solution to this very common Catholic problem. A while back, on her blog *The Snoring Scholar*, Sarah hosted a long group of posts under the heading "Looking Closer at the Hail Mary: The Complete Prayer." She invited Catholics from all over the place to contribute to this project that took each individual word (yes, even "of" and "the") and expanded on what that individual word within the prayer meant. This was all collected into a book from Ave Maria Press by the name of *Word by Word: Slowing Down with the Hail Mary*. If you take a good look at your engagement with this beautiful and biblical prayer and feel as if you've been going through the motions as of late, I suggest getting back on track via this book from Sarah.

PUTTING THE DIVINE OFFICE
TO WORK IN OUR LIVES

by Anna Mitchell

When it comes to prayer, the Liturgy of the Hours can be the perfect companion for the Catholic hipster. Some might not be aware that the Liturgy of the Hours is actually the official prayer of the Catholic Church. Priests, for instance, are not obligated to celebrate Mass every day (though they are certainly encouraged to do so), but they are required to pray the Hours—and the laity has been highly encouraged to pray them as well.

The Liturgy of the Hours is broken up into prayers that are to be said at different hours of the day: Morning Prayer, the Office of Readings, Midday Prayer, Evening Prayer, and Night Prayer. In spreading it out this way, the Church has ensured that her ministers fulfill the mandate of Jesus to pray without ceasing. And for all of us who take the time to pray even some of the Hours, this is a way to consecrate our time each day.

Each of the Hours is structured similarly. There's an optional opening hymn, recitation of the psalms (and sometimes canticles from other books of the Bible), a scripture reading, intercessions, and a closing prayer. The Office of Readings, believe it or not, has more reading involved—one reading from scripture and another from a saint—and so it takes a little bit longer, but all the others you can finish in about ten minutes or less.

Now, there are a number of philosophical and practical reasons why the Divine Office (as the Liturgy of the Hours is also called) is the perfect prayer regimen for the Catholic hipster. First of all, this is the vintage way to pray, going all the way back to Jesus himself—not to mention that the psalms are even more vintage than that. Second, it's a great way to pray with the community of believers without actually having to be around other people. Third, there's definitely an exciting insider aspect to knowing the ins and outs of how to use the ribbons and move about the Breviary (the book containing the Divine Office).

Speaking of the Breviary, you have several options. When it comes to the book version, you can get the full four-volume set, which includes all of the different prayers, psalms, and readings for various liturgical seasons, feast days, and whatnot. Then there is a condensed one-volume version called *Christian Prayer*, which is not comprehensive but covers the major stuff. If you're not quite so hip as to prefer the book version, there are also some apps you can download—the most popular being the iBreviary app or the Divine Office app. (For more, see "The Must-Have Apps," by Lisa M. Hendey, pages 80–84.) The advantage to these is that you don't have to worry about the ribbons nor do you have to be aware of what feast day or liturgical season it is (if you can call that an advantage).

COOL SAINT:
ST. BASIL THE GREAT

Though he is arguably just as important as St. Benedict in the development of monasticism, St. Basil does not come close to the name recognition that St. Benedict holds among Catholics in the West.

Basil was born in Caesarea to an incredibly holy family: his grandmother, both parents, and several of his siblings are all canonized saints. After spending some time in the world of academia, where he saw much success, he decided to become a monk and founded a monastery in modern-day Turkey. He wrote a monastic rule that earned him the reputation today of being for Eastern monasticism what St. Benedict was for Western monasticism. St. Basil founded several other monasteries before being ordained the bishop of Caesarea in 370 and becoming a great defender of orthodoxy against the Arian heresy.

St. Basil the Great, pray for us.

FORGOTTEN PRAYER

The Canticle of Zechariah (from Morning Prayer)

Blessed be the Lord,
the God of Israel;
he has come to his people and set them free.
He has raised up for us a mighty savior,
born of the house of his servant David.
Through his holy prophets he promised of old
that he would save us from our enemies,
from the hands of all who hate us.
He promised to show mercy to our fathers
and to remember his holy covenant.
This was the oath he swore to our father Abraham:
To set us free from the hands of our enemies,
free to worship him without fear,
holy and righteous in his sight
all the days of our life.
You, my child, shall be called

> the prophet of the Most High;
> for you will go before the Lord to prepare his way,
> to give his people knowledge of salvation
> by the forgiveness of their sins.
> In the tender compassion of our Lord
> the dawn from on high shall break upon us,
> to shine on those who dwell in darkness
> and the shadow of death,
> and to guide our feet into the way of peace.
> Glory to the Father and to the Son and to the Holy
>   Spirit:
> as it was in the beginning, is now, and will be for ever.
>   Amen.

ACTIVITY

Pray the Liturgy of the Hours. To start, download one of any number of apps to begin praying the Hours on your smartphone. Set alarms to remind yourself when to pray, and make it part of your daily routine. Some religious communities near you may invite the laity to join them for something such as Vespers (Evening Prayer) or Compline (Night Prayer)—make a point to go and participate with those who really know what they're doing.

DAILY MASS, DAILY MASS, DAILY MASS, DAILY MASS, DAILY MASS . . .

by Fr. Kyle Schnippel

One of my favorite memories when I was a child was serving daily Mass prior to heading off to school. Admittedly, for my Catholic-school-educated brethren, this is probably not that big of a deal; but I went to the local public school. Scheduling was not that great of an issue, as Mass was at 7:30 and school started at 8:00; we could just barely make it, and if we were late, "I was serving Mass" was always an acceptable excuse! Small-town Ohio for the win.

It wasn't just the ready excuse for tardiness at school, though, that makes this such a favorable memory. Before Mass, Fr. O'Connor would take time to talk with the servers, asking us questions about what was going on in our lives, explaining the various liturgical colors, and so on. It was an opportunity for us to get to know him as a person, not just as the Reverend Figure, the Priest.

Looking back now, those chats and conversations—those little moments of idle chitchat with Fr. O'Connor—were certainly seeds of my own vocation to the priesthood. Eventually, after I entered the seminary and was back at my home parish to help serve for Christmas or Holy Week, a fellow parishioner came up to me after Mass and said, "You looked just like Fr. O'Connor up there!" I walked home smiling, as that was the best compliment I think anyone could have given me at the time!

Now, after eleven-and-a-half years as a priest, daily Mass still remains a favorite. People are there who want to be there, who want to encounter Christ on that daily basis. The readings cover more of the Bible in a systematic way; especially during Ordinary Time, there are series of readings from the various books of the Bible. Long stretches of history are covered all at once; the letters of St. Paul are read through in order, for example. Plus, the chaos of daily life is silenced for those thirty minutes or so of prayer that occur during Mass—not to mention the calendar of saints that we get to encounter, too!

THE CYCLE OF READINGS

Unlike Sunday Masses—where the Old Testament reading is chosen in light of the gospel for that week and the New Testament reading is a series from (typically) a letter of St. Paul—in daily Masses, the normal course of readings for the first reading and the gospel is independent, especially during Ordinary Time.

For daily Mass readings in Ordinary Time (the normal cycle of readings assigned on each date, which you can find at the United States Conference of Catholic Bishops website, as opposed to readings assigned for particular feasts), every year, the three synoptic gospels of Matthew, Mark, and Luke are read pretty much in order, excluding the infancy and Passion narratives. This allows those who attend daily Mass, or even just follow along with the readings on a daily basis, to have a sense of the flow of each gospel: how Jesus moves and interacts with the crowds, how the level of tension continues to increase between him and the Jewish authorities, and so on. It also allows for the differences in each gospel to be highlighted slowly; for example, by the time we reach Luke, later in the calendar year, more and more women start to appear—ministering to and with Jesus.

While we hear the same gospel passages every year, the first reading for daily Mass is on a two-year cycle chosen to fit with the time of year and the seasons that we are going through, but it can also just be a long series of highlights from different parts of the Bible. So, for example, as we leave Christmastide and enter Ordinary Time, we hear from First and Second Samuel and First Kings before entering Lent. The stories of Saul, David, Solomon, and the other kings of Israel make for a good transitional period between the two great seasons of Advent/Christmas and Lent/Easter.

However, as we come to the end of the Church's liturgical cycle, we hear from the book of Daniel one year and the book of Revelation the next, as these two books are highly apocryphal and focus on the end times, which is the emphasis as we round out the year and begin again anew with the First Sunday of Advent.

In between, there are series of readings from the Pentateuch, the Wisdom literature, the letters of St. Paul, the prophets, and so on. While the whole breadth of the scriptures is not covered, attending daily Mass consistently over a two-year period will expose you to a wide swath of scripture and help you to understand how God's plan of salvation was inaugurated and enacted through time.

THE CALENDAR OF SAINTS

Another significant aspect of daily Mass for me as a priest is the ability to look at the calendar of saints who are celebrated throughout the year and to hold up these heroes of the faith as we encounter their feast days. By looking at them, we can see that they are not just important historical figures; they are also role models for us today of how to live out our own relationship with Jesus Christ in the midst of the world. And they continue to intercede and pray for us before God's throne in heaven.

As a preacher, I love to try to connect saints from previous ages to our own day. Especially with the ancient saints and martyrs, it can be fun to tell their stories in quick recaps and make a few connections between what they suffered and how they can then inspire us to strive for that same ideal.

For more modern saints, it can be an interesting challenge to see how they dealt with the changes that happened in the Church or in the culture and how they still made Jesus Christ the center of their lives. For example, we can be inspired by St. John Bosco, who lived during the time of the Industrial Revolution and worked with children and young people. And there are so many other saints in between then and now whom we can connect with and learn from. This reinforces the idea that in our pursuit of Jesus Christ, in our pursuit of becoming better disciples, in our pursuit of the perfection that we seek in him, we are never alone. The saints are there with us, rooting us on and helping us all to strive to be better in Christ.

Who is your patron, and when is he or she celebrated?

THIRTY MINUTES OF SILENCE

I'm going to let you in on a little secret here: if you ask a priest which is his least favorite Mass during the year, chances are he might actually say it's the Christmas Vigil Mass. In every parish where I have served, those first Masses on Christmas Eve are chaotic, loud, noisy, and bustling. Yes, we try to make the best of it and make every Mass an encounter with Christ, but sometimes the crowds make it very difficult.

Daily Mass, on the other hand, is far removed from the hustle and bustle. Rather, in many parishes, the music is toned down, the crowds are often much smaller, and the atmosphere of prayer is increased. For many who are able to make a habit of attending daily Mass, this small refuge of silence and prayer becomes a cornerstone of their days, and without that engaging time of reflection, the hustle and bustle can carry them away.

What is it about this thirty minutes of silence that can transform an entire day? For one, I think it is a chance simply to rest in the Lord and to know that he truly is there, every day. Receiving the Eucharist on a daily basis, too, gives us that closeness to Christ that strengthens our resolve to be with him forever. Plus, the readings and/or the designated saint can give us something to contemplate and pray over through the rest of the day. All of this is greatly needed in our world.

But how could I also forget the daily shot in the arm of grace? That daily dose of Christ into life can utterly transform the humdrum into something mysterious and uplifting. Even if you cannot go every day, to make a pattern of attending daily Mass once or twice a week can start to configure your heart ever more into a heart for Jesus. Take the chance, and join the daily Mass crew during the week, and your Sunday experience can go to new heights as well!

COOL SAINT:
VEN. SOLANUS CASEY

A Wisconsin native born to Irish immigrants, Solanus Casey was a simple priest and humble servant of God in the United States. At the age of twenty-one, he witnessed a murder while at work, which led him to reevaluate his life and focus on a call to the priesthood. Unable to complete studies for his native

Archdiocese of Milwaukee, he joined the Capuchin Friars in Detroit, Michigan, with the hope that he could one day become just a simplex priest, one who could preside and celebrate Mass but did not have faculties to preach or hear confessions. In 1904, at the age of twenty-two, he was ordained to the priesthood as just that.

After a series of assignments, he was eventually brought back to Detroit and spent twenty-one years at St. Bonaventure Monastery, where he primarily worked as a porter or door-keeper. He found a deep joy in being able to celebrate Mass, and even though there is evidence that he was granted full faculties as a priest, he never exercised them, preferring to stay as a simplex priest.

He saw his mission as bringing the grace and healing of God to the poor and the needy in his area and would simply welcome and comfort those who came to his door. Every Wednesday, he conducted services for the sick at the monastery. His compassion and empathy won many hearts to Christ and resulted in many healings through his intercession.

He passed to the next life on July 31, 1957, in Detroit, with his last words reportedly being, "I give my soul to Jesus Christ." On July 8, 1987, his body was exhumed and reinterred in the center that bears his name at the monastery that was his home for so long. In 1995, Pope John Paul II declared him venerable and opened his cause for canonization, which is ongoing. Many make pilgrimages to his shrine, even today.

His love for Christ, fostered in his simple celebration of the Eucharist, should be a shining example for us all!

FORGOTTEN PRAYER

In the revised Roman Missal, there is a selection of prayers at the end for both preparation for Mass and thanksgiving after Mass. Below is a prayer selection from St. Thomas Aquinas, the Angelic Doctor and great theologian on the Eucharist, for preparation for Mass.

> Almighty and everlasting God, behold I come to the Sacrament of Thine only-begotten Son, our Lord Jesus Christ: I come as one infirm to the physician of life, as one unclean to the fountain of mercy, as one blind to the light of everlasting brightness, as one poor and needy to the Lord of heaven and earth. Therefore I implore the abundance of Thy measureless bounty that Thou wouldst vouchsafe to heal my infirmity, wash my uncleanness, enlighten my blindness, enrich my poverty, and clothe my nakedness, that I may receive the Bread of Angels, the King of kings, the Lord of lords, with such reverence and humility, with such sorrow and devotion, with such purity and faith, with such purpose and intention as may be profitable to my soul's salvation. Grant unto me, I pray, the grace of receiving not only the Sacrament of our Lord's Body and Blood, but also the grace and power of the Sacrament. O most gracious God, grant me so to receive the Body of Thine only begotten Son, our Lord Jesus Christ, which he took from the Virgin Mary, as to merit to be incorporated into his mystical Body, and to be numbered amongst his members. O most loving Father, give me grace to behold forever Thy beloved Son with his face at last unveiled, whom I now purpose to receive under the sacramental veil here below. Amen.
>
> —St. Thomas Aquinas

ACTIVITY

Work daily Mass into your calendar, if at all possible. While many parishes (mine own included) only have one Mass slot a day, maybe at a time when you are not able to attend, there are often other parishes that have an evening Mass (or retreat centers or monasteries might offer Mass throughout the day). If you work in a downtown area of a major city, it's likely that there are parishes there that have Masses scheduled during lunchtime and prior to the evening commute. Attending daily Mass even just once a week can really help to bring a deeper connection between our day-to-day work and our spiritual lives, as we ask God to bless the work of our hands.

EUCHARISTIC ADORATION—REVIVED

by Tiffany Walsh

Growing up as a cradle Catholic, I do not remember learning anything about Eucharistic adoration. Of course, I put very little effort into my spiritual life, so this could explain a lot. I am certain that we were taught about the True Presence of Christ in the Eucharist in our religious-education classes, but unfortunately that piece of information did not truly sink in until I was in my twenties, when I finally took the time to examine my faith on my own and fell in love with it.

Jesus is truly present in the Eucharist. How could I not be in awe of this? Sure enough, when I found a group of Catholic twentysomethings to socialize with, they regularly went to eucharistic adoration. What is this activity of which they speak? I now knew that I was receiving Jesus when I went forward for Communion at Mass, but I had never been inside of an adoration chapel. I was in for a delightful surprise.

The silence inside of a church or chapel, with the Eucharist displayed in a monstrance, was unlike any I had experienced before. It was as if the air itself was palpably infused with Jesus' presence. The ambiance unfailingly lends itself to prayer.

I have never had a particularly long attention span, so I was not sure how I would do in quiet prayer for longer than a few minutes at a time. To my surprise, even Catholic girls with a significant lack of ability for contemplative prayer can find the peace of the exposed Eucharist conducive to centering one's thoughts. The expectant silence soothed my overactive mind and spirit, and I was able to converse with God in a way that I had not experienced before.

I also liked the option of stopping in to visit with Jesus outside of attending Mass, just whenever I needed a spiritual pick-me-up. Some churches have either perpetual or weekly times for eucharistic adoration, or they may simply leave the main sanctuary open and you may pray there with Jesus near you in the tabernacle. As you go about your daily tasks, sometimes these short visits yield remarkable spiritual comfort.

As a lifelong Catholic, I found eucharistic adoration to be a hidden gem. There was so much that I was discovering about my faith at this time, even from newer Catholics, and my own ignorance was humbling. Importantly, though, nothing was more rewarding than the spiritual solace I was finding in my new passion for my Catholic faith.

I am no longer in my twenties, but I find the joy of Jesus in the Eucharist just as fresh and new as I did then. That sensation of closeness, of intimacy, is quite timeless. Back then, I prayed at adoration for guidance on my vocation and for peace in my job environment, which I found quite stressful. Was I called to the religious life? Should I go back to school to pursue a different degree, something I found more meaningful? Was I called to work for the Church as a laywoman?

As I approached my thirties, I prayed about my job situation (again), since that had not improved, and I had discerned that I was not called to the religious life. Inside the shrine of Sainte-Anne-de-Beaupré in Quebec during an Advent pilgrimage one year, in front of Jesus in the tabernacle, I prayed to find a husband, if that was God's will for me. Indeed, in January of the following year, I met my future husband. I also quit my job to return to graduate school, and now I have a career as a librarian that I find very enjoyable and stress-free.

God's answers to our prayers are not necessarily always quick or clear (at first), but I have found that the greatest way to find peace in the meantime is to seek Jesus out in the Eucharist. He is always there, awaiting our visit to him. It is an invitation that we should seize wholeheartedly.

COOL SAINT:
ST. PETER JULIAN EYMARD

St. Peter Julian Eymard was born in southern France in 1811. As a young man, he enjoyed working under the apprenticeship of his father, a knife maker, as well as pursuing his own interest in the priesthood. After he became an adult, he was ordained in his hometown diocese of Grenoble and served in several parishes there. He later joined the Marists and was a member of that community for nearly twenty years. During his time there, St. Peter Julian developed a great love for Jesus truly present in the Eucharist. He frequently preached about the Eucharist and about the Forty Hours devotion of eucharistic exposition. Later, he founded a new religious order totally devoted to the Eucharist, which became known as the Congregation of the Blessed Sacrament. His order was approved by the bishops of Paris in 1856.

Within his new community, St. Peter Julian worked with his brother priests to prepare children for First Communion and to bring nonpracticing Catholics back into the traditions and sacraments of their faith—particularly reception of the sacrament of Reconciliation and the Eucharist. He was a vocal proponent of laypeople and religious alike receiving the Eucharist as frequently as possible.

St. Peter Julian died in 1868 at age fifty-seven from complications following a stroke. He was beatified in 1925 and canonized in 1962 in the midst of the Second Vatican Council. His feast day is August 2.

St. Peter Julian Eymard, pray for us.

FORGOTTEN PRAYER

The Extended Our Father

Our Father Who art in Heaven . . .
Hallowed be Your Name

> first in myself, through the spirit of Your humility, obedience, and charity. May I in all humility and zeal make You known, loved and adored by all men in the Holy Eucharist.

Thy Kingdom come

> Thy Eucharistic kingdom. Rule forever over us for Your greater glory through the power of Your love, the triumph of Your virtues and the grace of a Eucharistic vocation in my state as a layman. Grant me the grace of Your love so that I may be able to effectively extend Your Eucharistic kingdom everywhere and realize the desire You expressed: "I have come to cast fire on the earth; and what will I, but that it be kindled!" O that I might be the incendiaries of this heavenly fire!

Thy Will be done on earth as it is in Heaven

> Grant me the grace to find all my joy in wanting You alone, in desiring You alone and in thinking of You alone. Grant that by denying myself, I may find light and life in obeying Your good, acceptable and perfect Will. I will what You will. I will it because You will it. I will it as You will it. I will it as long as You will it. Keep my thoughts and desires purely from You, for You and in You.

Give us this day our daily bread

You are our Eucharistic Lord and You alone will
be my food and clothing, my riches and glory, my
remedy in illness and my protection against all evil.
You will be all things to me.
And forgive us our trespasses . . .
As we forgive those who trespass against us . . .
And lead us not into temptation but deliver us from
   evil
   Deliver me Jesus, from the demon of pride, impu-
   rity, discord and complacency. Deliver me from the
   cares and worries of life so that with a pure heart
   and a free mind I may joyfully spend my life and
   devote all that I am and all that I have in the service
   of You my Eucharistic Lord.
Amen.[15]

—St. Peter Julian Eymund

ACTIVITY

Here are five spirit-focusing activities for adorers with short
attention spans.

- Read—This is coming from a bookworm librarian, so I suppose it
  is somewhat self-serving. Reading, however, is an excellent way
  to settle one's mind in the presence of the Eucharist. One option
  is the Bible—I do not know about you, but I can never stick to a
  consistent Bible reading schedule! Adoration is the perfect quiet
  spot to dive in. Other options include one of the spiritual classics,
  such as *Introduction to the Devout Life* by St. Francis de Sales, *Story
  of a Soul* by St. Thérèse of Lisieux, or an inspiring collection of
  conversion stories.
- Pray the Rosary—I often try to pray the Rosary in the car, but
  I find that my meditation on the mysteries is constantly inter-
  rupted by my need to signal a right turn or stop suddenly for a
  traffic jam. Adoration is the perfect place to give the mysteries

more attention, even if you are only able to get through a single decade rather than a full Rosary.

- Pray a chaplet—The possibilities here are endless. There are chaplet prayers out there focused on specific devotions to our Lord (Divine Mercy, the Sacred Heart of Jesus), to our Lady under particular titles (Undoer of Knots, Star of the Sea), and to saints (St. Kateri Tekakwitha, St. Thérèse, St. Monica), to mention only a few. Chaplets usually include fewer prayers than the Rosary and can be prayed quite quickly.

- Slowly repeat a short invocation prayer—This could be something as simple as praying, "Lord Jesus, have mercy on me, a sinner," or "Lord, be with me now." I find repetition to be incredibly soothing and meditative, and it is much easier for my mind to slip into a contemplative state, conducive to quiet reflection, when I focus on repeated words.

- Sit for five minutes and speak with God in your heart, as if you were talking to a friend—In other words, have a conversation. I find conversational prayer to be intimidating, and thus having a general time frame helps me to just relax and begin. The Lord is waiting for us; we only need to seize the quiet invitation.

HANGING WITH PRIESTS?

by Fr. Kyle Schnippel

When I was growing up in a small town in western Ohio, big families were fairly common. We thought it was perfectly normal to be in a family of six children; after all, there were families of eight, nine, or eleven children in town, too. Because we had lots of cousins as well, this made going to my grandma and grandpa's on my mom's side of the family so much fun; there were a ton of other kids around to play with! On Dad's side, it was typically just us, since our cousins lived out of town.

By the time I was in high school, my oldest sisters started their own families, and there have been little people around at family gatherings since then. As a fairly strong extrovert, I find being in big crowds entertaining and refreshing, at least for a little while.

But now, as with many priests, I'm a little ways away from my family and do not get to see them as often as I would like, so I lean on other friends to fill some of that need to be with people and to find the joy that comes from walking with others on their paths of life. Plus, as is the case with many priests these days, I live alone and face the trials of ministering to two (or more) parish communities. There are unique stresses that get placed on us; and this is where it becomes important for the priest to have a wide variety of friends and acquaintances.

Our Lord faced this, too! In the beginning of Luke 8, we see Jesus journeying and ministering throughout the region of Galilee, proclaiming the kingdom of God. "Accompanying him were the Twelve and some women who had been cured of evil spirits and infirmities, Mary, called Magdalene, from whom seven demons had gone out, Joanna, the wife of Herod's steward Chuza, Susanna, and many others who provided for them out of their resources" (Lk 8:1b–3).

Jesus understands the need for companionship and friendship. In his journeys and ministering, he has several levels of friendship: even among the Twelve, it seems that Peter, James, and John were his closest friends and confidants. The rest of the Twelve were with him on a nearly consistent basis. In Luke's gospel, we see that Jesus sends out seventy or seventy-two other disciples in ministry (see Luke 10).[16] The women mentioned above, seemingly both single and married women, also journey with him, plus all those who encounter him at various points during their own journeys: Zaccheaus and Simon of Cyrene, for example.

In all of this, we see the importance of friendship. Even our Lord recognizes that while the mission of salvation is uniquely his, he freely shares that mission and needs the assistance of others to fully bring it about. If it is true for Jesus, it is certainly true for priests today as well.

In talking to my friends on this topic, I asked them about some of the benefits of having priest friends around. It was fun to hear from their perspectives:

- Mass intentions—The grace of the celebration of the Eucharist is unlimited and should not be wasted! Especially on days off, I sometimes look around for various intentions to apply to the Mass I celebrate privately. If no family needs are pressing, I will often include friends in my intentions, especially if I know they are facing a particular struggle or have shared with me something that needs prayer and guidance. It is my hope that by doing so, they might have some clarity in moving forward and finding the path that God has laid out for them in whatever situation.

- Comfort at Mass—This one surprised me. I recently completed a three-month sabbatical (some time off for prayer and reflection). After my first Sunday Mass back at my parish, some friends said, "It feels like home again." It was interesting to me as the priest that just my presence made friends (and parishioners!) feel more comfortable at Mass. It shows to me the family nature of "priest as father" in leading the community in prayer.

- Conversations can become spiritual direction—Let's face it; as priests we have lots of training and experience to help people through difficulties in life—not just parishioners who stop by the office but also friends with whom we are just hanging out. One of my hobbies is home brewing; that's when I often invite friends over to hang out and just chat. There is enough to do while brewing that things do not get boring, but there is also lots of free time to bring up the matters of the day or week, just to see how Jesus is in the midst of a particular topic. I often laugh that priests certainly never have boring conversations because we can always bring the topic to a deeper level.

These are just a few of the hidden benefits of hanging out with priests, and I am sure you can think of a few more. Overall, I think it is good for both the priest and his friends that these friendships develop. However, there are also some things to be aware of from the priest's point of view that can be difficult.

- Confidentiality—There are things we just cannot discuss. Admittedly, this could probably be the case on both sides of this ledger. We are trained to keep secrets. As such, there are topics and times when friends ask me certain things, and I just look and say,

"Can't go there." Because of a friend's desire to be compassionate and help me process whatever that topic is, I can see that it has, at times, been hurtful to the friend that I can't discuss it. But on the flip side, I am hopeful that it brings them some solace in knowing that when they are on the other side of the issue, I will keep their secrets, too.

- Interruptions—When the phone rings, sometimes we just need to go. I have been hosting gatherings at the rectory when an unexpected call has come in for an emergency anointing, and off I've had to go. Most of the time, it has not been an issue. I'll run to the hospital and let everyone hang around; every once in a while, I have had to call a party short because of the phone call. Alas, it is part of the territory.

- Schedules—As a pastor, it can be challenging to find time to get together. (Working weekends is a real drag!) Nearly every evening sees some sort of meeting and/or appointment, if not several. Finding time to get together with friends takes some planning and forethought; it is rare that I can get a text message with a "Let's go to dinner this evening!" and respond with "Time and place?" Too often, it is a "No can do; I have x, y, and z this evening. :(" Most of my friends understand this and try to be as accommodating as possible to the craziness that is scheduling these days. And when I feel sorry for myself, I talk to my sisters who have five children each and realize that my calendar isn't so bad after all!

We talk of parishes as families of faith—and the pastor as the head of that family. To be friendly with your priest can be a great asset in his exercising of his ministry. When he has to make difficult decisions, it is helpful to know that at least some of his parishioners will support and back him.

And more important than anything is to pray for him. Pray that he will be a good and worthy shepherd after the heart of the Good Shepherd. His holiness and virtue will assist all of his parishioners to strive for that same holiness and virtue.

May we all walk together toward the Lord!

COOL SAINT:
ST. LYDIA PURPURARIA

As Paul traveled during his missionary journeys, he encountered many who were God-fearing and who helped him along the way, allowing him to stay with them, work with them, and take advantage of their hospitality. One such person was St. Lydia Purpuraria in Acts 16:13b–15: "We sat and spoke with the women who had gathered there. One of them, a woman named Lydia, a dealer in purple cloth, from the city of Thyatira, a worshiper of God, listened, and the Lord opened her heart to pay attention to what Paul was saying. After she and her household had been baptized, she offered us an invitation, 'If you consider me a believer in the Lord, come and stay at my home,' and she prevailed on us."

Not much else is known about her. She seems to have been fairly well off as a dealer of purple cloth (a mark of royalty or wealth in that time). But what we can see from this small exchange is that she assisted Paul in his missionary work and provided him with a place to stay. I wonder what conversations they had as he went about his work?

Perhaps one of the biggest challenges of being friends with a priest is having to stand by and watch him do his work—having to be content to stand on the side until he is done ministering to others. Hopefully, St. Lydia's example in prevailing upon St. Paul that he stay with her and her family may give comfort to all in a similar situation.

FORGOTTEN PRAYER

Prayer for Priests

O Almighty and Eternal God, look upon the Face of Thy Christ, and for love of Him Who is the eternal High-priest, have pity on Thy priests. Remember, O most compassionate God, that they are but weak and frail human beings. Stir up in them the grace of their vocation which is in them by the imposition of the Bishop's hands. Keep them close to Thee, lest the enemy prevail against them, so that they may never do anything in the slightest degree unworthy of their sublime vocation.

O Jesus, I pray Thee for Thy faithful and fervent priests; for Thy unfaithful and tepid priests; for Thy priests laboring at home or abroad in distant mission fields; for Thy tempted priests; for Thy lonely and desolate priests; for Thy young priests; for Thy aged priests; for Thy sick priests; for Thy dying priests; for the souls of Thy priests in Purgatory.

But above all I commend to Thee the priests dearest to me: the priest who baptized me; the priests at whose Masses I assisted and who gave me Thy Body and Blood in Holy Communion; the priests who taught and instructed or helped me and encouraged me; all the priests to whom I am indebted in any other way, particularly (*your priest's name here*). O Jesus, keep them all close to Thy heart, and bless them abundantly in time and in eternity. Amen. Mary, Queen of the clergy, pray for us; obtain for us many and holy priests. Amen.

—Richard Cardinal Cushing
(1895–1970)
Archbishop of Boston

ACTIVITY

Learn your pastor's or priest's vocation story: When did he hear the call to seminary formation? What seminary did he attend, and why that particular seminary and not another? Were there any obstacles that he had to overcome during his time of formation? What previous assignments has he had? Take all that information, and make him a "Patron Saint" wall: find the patron saints of all the parishes he has served in, and assemble icons or drawings; present them to him as recognition of his journey through the priesthood.

PART FOUR
REDISCOVER THE ATTRACTION

There's something inexplicably attractive, spiritually speaking, about someone who is on fire for the Catholic faith and working hard to live a life in accordance with the teachings and understanding of the Church.

From talking about your personal experience of God's mercy to being willing to stand out in a crowd that will categorize you as "different," from kneeling before the bones of people who actually met Jesus while he walked on this world to finding the breath of fresh air coming from a television sitcom with strong Catholic themes—there is quite a bit attractive about the Catholic faith.

We have the answer to what is ailing this world. We have the solutions to the many problems we find as we walk through this valley of tears. There's something attractive about our Catholic faith, and it's about time we rediscovered it.

GOD'S ABUNDANT MERCY

by Leticia Ochoa Adams

Mercy has been a theme in my life since my conversion in 2010. I lived a life entrenched in every sin imaginable except for murder, and that one is tricky because I knew a few friends who decided to have abortions and I did nothing to try and stop them. I began to have sex at the age of fourteen, and I was promiscuous for the next twenty years of my life. I was in and out of jail; I was a drunk; and I was full of anger and bitterness.

When I walked into St. William Catholic parish to begin RCIA classes, it was only to get my Catholic badge so my live-in boyfriend would marry me. I didn't want to get married because marriage was a sign of eternity or because it was a promise to my spouse and God to love him in a Christlike way. I wanted to marry him because I felt entitled to a wedding and wanted to prove to his ex-wife that I was better than she was. I had no intention of changing anything about my life, much less becoming a practicing Catholic. I really had no intention of making Jesus the Lord of my life. Been there, done that, and it was not for me.

I had a plan. That plan had everything to do with making my dreams come true and nothing to do with God. God, on the other hand, had his own plans, and he had an entire group of people in place to help him carry it out. They did so by meeting me where I was and not lecturing me about all the things that I was doing all wrong.

One of those people was Noe Rocha. Noe had been a heroin addict who got clean and fell in love with Jesus in 1977, the year that I was born. When I heard him talk about how God loved me, I knew that he was telling the truth. I knew in the depths of my soul that God was asking me to come back to him. Noe looked right in my direction and said, "God loves you more than you think he does; no matter what you have done, no matter how far you have gone, he loves you." I sat in my car for twenty minutes after class and cried. I had no clue why.

The next day I went to the parish office to register my children for RCIA adapted for children and filled out the parish registration form. I was really angry, and I had no idea why. I just knew that these judgmental church people were going to tell me that I was a sinner. I already knew it. But instead, the lady who took my form smiled at me and was incredibly kind. Then she said that I needed to talk to Noe, so I followed her to the break room. When Noe came in, he asked me why I wanted to register my kids for sacraments. I told him what happened the night before and how I had cried in my car for a long time. He looked me right in the eye and told me, "God touched your heart; that's what happened." It never occurred to me that God had been talking to me or reaching out to me. I felt as if I was too far gone for that kind of thing.

For the next nine months, I argued about everything Noe taught in class. Mostly I argued about all the sex stuff, because I was convinced that the Catholic Church didn't know one thing about the reality of sexuality. I went to my first Confession with a newly ordained priest. When I sat down in his office, all the anger came flooding back out of nowhere. I was just angry that anyone would dare call me a sinner, but this priest didn't call me that. He listened to me and let me spew out all my sins angrily with all my justifications, and he did nothing but tell me that God loved me. That priest became one of my closest friends and spiritual mentors. He taught me how to read the *Catechism* and papal documents. When I argued with something that the Church taught, he didn't grow impatient; he just listened and then sent me on a quest to read the reasons why the Church teaches what she does.

Both Noe and Fr. J., along with many other people at my parish, poured mercy into me. They didn't once make me feel as if I was somehow less than they were. Never did anyone call me out on my sins; instead they all loved me, *taught* me, and let me come to the realization about what were my sins. They helped me encounter Christ, and he did the heavy lifting to allow me to see what sin was and how it applied in my life.

When I looked at Noe and Father, I saw two men who loved Jesus. They both knew him as a person, not as an idea. Jesus wasn't a concept they just brought up as a cliché, but they had a relationship with him and loved him; through them, I came to know Jesus too, which made the changes I was making in my life not about rules but about a relationship.

It was obvious to me that Jesus loved them both in a real way. I wanted that. Because of how I was received by the people at my parish with mercy first and foremost, I could open my heart to Christ, and I fell in love with him. From that place of deep love, I came to accept, believe, and be obedient to the Church's teachings.

When things get difficult (and they do), I know where to find my Beloved. When I fail to love or be merciful to others, I throw myself at God's mercy in Confession. He has never turned me away. My conversion was a work of God's mercy. I know that he is Mercy itself, because I am here and I know him personally.

COOL SAINT:
ST. TERESA OF CALCUTTA

Mother Teresa was a great example of a person who lived out the vocation of mercy. One of my favorite quotations of hers is, "If you judge people, you will have no time to love them." It's my favorite not because I think that there are never things that people do that need to be judged. Mother Teresa was aware of the need to call things right or wrong—just listen to her speeches on topics such as abortion. But what she meant was that when we question people's motives, we waste time that we could be using to help them. When people came to her, she didn't spend time asking them why they were in the situations they were in—if they were hungry, she fed them; if they were thirsty, she gave them drink; if they were dying, she held them in her arms and comforted them. That is mercy in action.

In the story of the prodigal son, the father goes out to meet his son and calls the servants to put sandals on the young man's feet and to get ready for the party. He rejoiced and hugged his son because he was so happy to have his child back. He didn't interrogate the son at all. He didn't ask him anything; he just loved him. I am sure that at some point, they had a long talk about the son's actions, but at that moment, the father just simply loved. That is what mercy is.

Mercy can't be earned, and none of us deserve it. Jesus never said, "Make sure that you are only merciful to those who deserve it." He said to feed the hungry, give drink to the thirsty, and clothe the naked simply because those in need are his children; we all are. It is much easier to reach out to people we know and love because we consider them to be worthy, but mercy goes so much deeper than that.

St. Teresa of Calcutta taught us how deep mercy goes and how it can change the world, a little bit at a time.

FORGOTTEN PRAYER

A Morning Prayer

O my God! I offer Thee all my actions of this day for the intentions and for the glory of the Sacred Heart of Jesus. I desire to sanctify every beat of my heart, my every thought, my simplest works, by uniting them to Its infinite merits; and I wish to make reparation for my sins by casting them into the furnace of Its Merciful Love.

O my God! I ask of Thee for myself and for those whom I hold dear, the grace to fulfill perfectly Thy Holy Will, to accept for love of Thee the joys and sorrows of this passing life, so that we may one day be united together in heaven for all Eternity. Amen.

—St. Thérèse of Lisieux[17]

ACTIVITY

Call up those you disagree with—or e-mail or text them—and ask them out for coffee, drinks, or dinner to just have fun. Do not talk about any of those things that you disagree about, but find common ground, the common ground that has these people in your life in the first place, and talk about that. Just enjoy their company as human beings. See Jesus in them as Mother Teresa saw Jesus in those whom she helped. Meet them where they are; enjoy them for who they are and not who you want them to be. That is how God enjoys your company.

STANDING OUT IN A CROWD [OF MOSTLY PROTESTANTS]

by Arleen Spenceley

During my second week as a student at a private school, my teacher stood in front of the chalkboard, behind a podium, with a straight face and a noble mission: to ensure the eternal salvation of her entire fifth-grade class.

I sat with wide eyes and probably folded hands as she made a bold declaration: "It's a lot easier for Protestants to get to heaven than it is for Catholics."

This concerned me for two reasons: first, because I was a Catholic, and second, because I had a question that I did not dare ask out loud: "What the heck is a Protestant?"

I was ten years old and egocentric. Until the moment my teacher spoke the word "Protestant," I thought all people were either Catholics or Jews (my mom's side of the family is Catholic and my dad's is Jewish, but here I was a student in a Protestant private school). In a single fell swoop, my teacher taught me that Protestants exist and that I dang well better be one, lest my path likely lead straight to hell.

I raised my hand.

"I'm Catholic," I declared, in a tone not yet as bold as hers.

"Uh . . . that's OK," she said, clearly startled. And then she changed the subject.

The experience confused me, at first. I did not know yet that it would fuel me. So I said the Sinner's Prayer that night—a plea to the Lord to get inside my heart and stay there, just in case my teacher turned out to be right. Then I told my parents what she said.

My dad, who quite conveniently was then a catechumen in our parish's RCIA program, broke out the big guns: the Bible, the *Catechism*, and an impressive collection of Scott Hahn cassette tapes. It marked the start of a season of my childhood in which I dug, out of necessity, into what the Catholic Church actually teaches.

This would change my life.

But it would complicate life for the Protestant teachers and staff at my school—those whose smiles usually smacked of shock or mischief (i.e., "You're Catholic? This should be fun.").

And it was, straight through my senior year of high school.

Ordinarily, we wore uniforms (khakis and polos; let's not get crazy). But we could pay a couple of bucks on occasional Fridays to wear jeans and our favorite Christian T-shirts. In big, white letters, one of mine listed the top ten reasons to be Roman Catholic. (It scandalized the math teacher, who insisted she read it aloud.)

We had history books with chapters devoted to calling Catholics out for worshiping Mary and the saints (for the hundredth time, folks: *we don't*). I am pretty sure I wrote *false* and *nope* in all the margins. As a sophomore, I also made an appointment on that subject with the principal.

"Read this," I said as I handed him a copy of my history book, open to a page with lies about what Catholics believe highlighted in yellow.

He read it.

"And now, read this," I said, and I handed him a copy of the Nicene Creed.

He read that, too.

"Now tell me," I said, "where in this," I pointed at the Creed, "do you see that?" I pointed at the history book.

"Nowhere," he said.

The next academic year, the school had a new history curriculum.

I can't forget, though, the teacher who collected anti-Catholic comic books and displayed them on a bookshelf in his classroom. I read one of them during a study hall.

"I think my mom would like to read this," I said. "May I borrow it?"

"Yes," he said, and I shoved it into my book bag. The bell rang, and I darted for the door.

"Wait," the teacher said. "Is your mom Catholic?"

"Yes," I said. "And so am I."

I smiled and left the room. The anti-Catholic comics were banned from the campus shortly after.

I endured—nay, enjoyed—these (and many other related) experiences until my high school graduation. And yes, they were fun. And they were challenging. And they were irritating. My parents even gave me the option to return to public school. But I didn't. And today I wouldn't change that.

These experiences are in part what made me who I am. They kept me Catholic.

To interact consistently for eight years with people who didn't believe what I believe and to learn to do so mostly civilly was invaluable. It inspired the guts to study what the Church teaches instead of accepting what my teachers and books told me as if it were truth. It inspired the guts to speak up—to say, "You don't get to tell me what my Church teaches. I get to tell you!"

And it inspired the guts to stand out—to meet Christ through Catholicism, and to live out and share what the Church teaches as best I can, even if surrounded by a crowd of people who don't like it.

COOL SAINT: ST. NATALIA

St. Natalia—also spelled St. Nathalia—was a Muslim convert to Christianity. She and her husband, St. Aurelius, also a convert, at first continued to practice Muslim traditions in public and Christianity in private. Their new faith was not accepted by the majority that surrounded them—in fact, people who practiced it were persecuted.

It's written that once Aurelius "saw a Christian merchant being publicly beaten for stating that Islam was a false religion, and this made him think about his own cowardice in hiding his religious beliefs."[18] So he and St. Natalia decided to live out their faith openly from then on. Their decision to do so resulted in the conversions of their family members Felix and George (who are also now saints) and, eventually, in their imprisonment and martyrdom.

St. Natalia is my Confirmation saint. I chose her because, as a Catholic at a Protestant school, in a small way, I could relate.

FORGOTTEN PRAYER

Almighty, ever-living God, you conferred on Sts. Nathalia, Aurelius, Felix, and George the grace to suffer for Christ. Extend your divine help also to our weakness, so that just as they never shrank from dying for you, we may remain steadfast in our confession of you. Amen.

ACTIVITY

Study the Dialogue Institute's "Dialogue Principles," and practice them when your Protestant friends ask questions about
Catholicism. The Principles, formerly known as the "Dialogue
Decalogue," offer a set of ground rules for discussing concepts
with people who don't believe what you do. I didn't learn them
until after I graduated from my Protestant school. But if I had
learned them sooner, I wouldn't have been irritated by the dis-
cussions I had with my Protestant teachers; I would have been
enriched by them. My favorite of the Principles are "One must
compare only her/his ideals with their partner's ideals and
her/his practice with the partner's practice, not one's ideals
with one's partner's practice" and "Each participant needs to
describe her/himself. For example, only a Muslim can describe
what it really means to be an authentic member of the Muslim
community."[19] For the sake of your blood pressure, read all the
Principles before you next discuss your faith with a Protestant.

BONES AND OTHER BITS: YES, RELICS!

by Tommy Tighe

Whenever I hear someone make a joke about how silly it is that Catholics pray to Mary, have statues of famous saints, or believe in purgatory, I always think to myself, "Obviously, you haven't heard about relics!" Because how could anyone suggest that anything is weirder about Catholics than our veneration of relics?

My family had an opportunity a number of years back to venerate the femur bone of St. Mary Magdalene while her relic made a tour stop at St. Michael's Abbey in Silverado, California. Of course, as weirdo Catholics, we jumped at the opportunity, and we still look back on it as one of the coolest things we've ever seen.

I mean, there we were, standing before the femur bone of the first person to see Jesus after he had risen from the tomb. It's almost too crazy to believe.

We are surrounded by a great cloud of witnesses, and as Catholics we go to great lengths to show how grateful we are for their example, their prayers, and their accompaniment. The lives of the saints are like road maps to guide us all on our own faith walks, and venerating the saints (and their bones) seems to be a great way to show God how appreciative we are for the way he worked through them.

Now that's not to say that it isn't also a bit weird.

When non-Catholics trot out their typical arguments against the faith, I try my best to be always ready to defend the hope that is within me. Purgatory? I'm ready. Praying to Mary? Bring it on. Papal infallibility? Just try me.

Relics?

Okay, I'll give them that one. It's a bit odd. And yet it also feels completely natural at the same time.

COOL SAINT: ST. SPYRIDON

St. Spyridon was born in Cyprus. He was a shepherd who married and had a daughter. Upon the death of his spouse, he entered the monastery and eventually wound up as bishop of Trimuthous. As unusual as it was at the time, he peacefully died in old age in the year 348.

When the Arab armies took Cyprus, Spyridon's body was disinterred and taken to Constantinople. Amazingly, his relics were found to be incorrupt, and even better, smelling of basil. I'm a huge fan of basil and could practically eat pesto by the spoonful, but back in the day, basil was considered a royal plant, which pretty much solidified Spyridon's greatness. His relics continue to be taken in procession every Palm Sunday and on other special occasions.

FORGOTTEN PRAYER

A Prayer before Relics from the Shrine of the Holy Relics

Oh, saints of God, in faith and confidence I turn my prayers to you. I am told that these relics are portions of your earthly remains. These relics call to mind your lives of virtue, your lives dedicated to the love of Christ and of his holy Gospel.

I ask your prayers on this, my pilgrimage. I pray that you may join as one great choir asking our loving Father to assist me in my life, to help me find the path to holiness, to a life filled with virtue and love.

All you holy children of the Father, who are a great strength to the Church, bless me with your prayers. I give praise to our Father for your lives of faith and courage, for your love and devotion. I offer thanksgiving for your example to the world and your prayers for me. Amen.[20]

ACTIVITY

Sit back, close your eyes, and allow your mind to focus.

Consider an alternate universe where you have attained sainthood, and those who honor you and ask for your intercession long to venerate a relic of yours to help connect them more closely with you. If you got to pick what kind of relic it was, what would you select? A bone fragment? A used handkerchief? A dusty, old rosary that you used on a daily basis? What would it be?

BEING FANS OF EACH OTHER

by Lisa M. Hendey

President John F. Kennedy is credited with having popularized the phrase, "A rising tide lifts all boats." While the phrase was originally intended to refer to socioeconomic ramifications, I often think of it in conjunction with the teachings of a man-God who once walked on water during a pretty wild tide.

In the Sermon on the Mount, Jesus calls out the hypocrites in the crowd, saying, "Why do you notice the splinter in your brother's eye, but do not perceive the wooden beam in your own eye?" (Mt 7:3). How easy it is for us people of faith to look at the world around us through the prism of our *Catechism*-colored spectacles and find fault with everyone but ourselves. Ask anyone who is active at your parish, and you'll find wildly varied perspectives on the holiness of everything from holding hands during the Our Father to which political candidates are most "Catholic."

All too often, in our desire to live as holy men and women, we slip into the sin of seeing fault in the world around us instead of focusing on our own spiritual journeys and shortcomings.

Don't get me wrong: I'm not suggesting that we ease our standards when it comes to living as people of faith. I'm simply suggesting that Jesus surrounded himself with disciples and that he called them to always err on the side of love. Were those closest to Christ perfect? Far from it! They argued among themselves and tried to curry his favor. They denied Jesus in his moment of greatest need. They hid. They doubted.

But when the Holy Spirit descended upon them, they were emboldened in a miraculous way that continues to bear fruit in Christ's Church. Read the epistles, and you will find spiritual leadership intent upon building up and teachers who have given themselves fully to affirming, edifying, and sending.

You and I are called to no less. While to like has been redefined too often these days as an action on social media, to love as Christ calls us to do means lifting one another up and grasping for God's love in unison. A Catholic hipster doesn't get more hip by dragging those around her down into the mud. She's perhaps closest to God when she lowers herself into it in the service of others.

As an object lesson, we can look to the life of St. Teresa of Calcutta. When we are tempted to look at others with derision, competition, or judgment, we can follow the example of she who said, "If you judge people, you will have no time to love them." Mother Teresa's secret to loving people was always seeing Christ in the faces of those she served. When we examine those around us with eyes oriented toward noticing Jesus in them, we begin to crave true connections.

Mercy calls us not only to forgive and forbear but to love our neighbors at every juncture. And being a part of the true Communion of Saints means recognizing that in loving, supporting, and living in union with one another, we ourselves are never lessened or diminished. Rather, we are built up, buoyed for the moments when our own holiness or spiritual strength is not sufficient for the challenges we find along our journeys.

In the words of the Doxology, we have a hymn of praise that calls us to a totally cool unity of purpose:

Through him, and with him, and in him, O God, almighty Father, in the unity of the Holy Spirit, all glory and honor is yours, forever and ever. Amen.

When we truly live united through, with, and in God, we rise together toward him.

COOL SAINT: ST. JOHN XXIII

While his rise to become one of the preeminent clerics of the twentieth century belies his simple roots as the eldest son of a farmer, a look at the life of the man who was born Angelo Giuseppe Roncalli points to a thread of bridge building, mediation, and a search for commonality in faith. Pope John Paul II once said of St. John XXIII, "Everyone remembers the image of Pope John's smiling face and two outstretched arms embracing the whole world. How many people were won over by his simplicity of heart, combined with a broad experience of people and things!"[21] As he rose through the ranks to the papacy, he gave his life to reforms on behalf of those most in need. He was a noted peacemaker who advocated for Jewish lives amid the terror of the Nazis. "Good Pope John's" encyclical *Pacem in Terris,* or "Peace on Earth," remains timely in today's wartorn world. This spiritual shepherd who interceded during the Cuban missile crisis also called for and convened the Second Vatican Council. While never wealthy in material goods, the patron saint of papal delegates is a natural go-to intercessor for those of us who believe that getting along trumps getting ahead.

FORGOTTEN PRAYER

After receiving the Eucharist, we pray the *Anima Christi.* In this moment, through our reception of the Real Presence of Christ in the Eucharist, we are fully united not only with Jesus but also with one another as brothers and sisters in Christ.

Soul of Christ, sanctify me.
Body of Christ, save me.
Blood of Christ, inebriate me.
Water from Christ's side, wash me.
Passion of Christ, strengthen me.
O good Jesus, hear me.
Within Thy wounds hide me.
Suffer me not to be separated from Thee,
From the malicious enemy defend me.
In the hour of my death call me,
And bid me come unto Thee,
That I may praise Thee with Thy saints
and with Thy angels
Forever and ever. Amen.

ACTIVITY

Use your digital footprint this week to build up the kingdom
of God. Start with your own parish social media platform by
leaving a kind and supportive comment on your parish's Facebook page. Next, leave a positive review for your parish on
Yelp, Google, Trip Advisor, or other online venues where new
friends might be looking for a church. Finally, thank whomever handles communications for your parish, and pray about
volunteering for or starting a digital-evangelization ministry
team in your parish community.

PRAYING TO YOUR BODYGUARD

by Sr. Brittany Harrison

Guardian angels are fairly popular in mainstream culture. The Catholic Church has a long history of devotion to them, with Jesus even reminding us in Matthew 18:10 to have a deep respect for children, because "their angels in heaven always look upon the face of my heavenly Father." If Jesus takes angels so seriously, perhaps we need to give them a fair consideration, as well.

Every person has an angel specifically chosen by God to guard and direct him or her during life on earth. This angel is not the soul of a deceased person but a distinct creation of God, appointed just for the person to whom the angel is assigned in order to help that individual grow in holiness. If the person chooses to love God and directs his or her choices to embracing the call to be an heir of the heavenly kingdom, the angel will remain with that person for all eternity.

It's a great blessing to have a guardian angel, and Catholic tradition teaches that parishes and even countries have angels assigned to guard them and the people within them. Some theologians and saints have even said that priests and people in positions of leadership have extra angels assigned to them to specifically help them in their ministries. We can see from this that angels are an essential part of God's plan of salvation.

Angels are spiritual persons, meaning that they have no physical bodies—thus the question that is sometimes posed, "How many angels can dance on the head of a pin?" is irrelevant since only physical bodies take up physical space and dancing is the action of a physical body. Since angels are pure spirit, they are not limited by physical space in the same way that we humans with physical bodies are, so at the same time they can behold the unveiled face of God and be present with us. This is not to say, however, that angels cannot take on a physical appearance (and even dance, if they so desire) for a limited time, such as when the archangel Raphael, in the book of Tobit, accompanied Tobias on his journey or when the archangel Gabriel in the Gospels of Matthew and Luke appeared to the Blessed Virgin Mary at the Annunciation.

St. John Bosco reminds us: "Be good. This will make your angel happy. When sorrows and misfortunes, physical or spiritual, afflict you, turn to your guardian angel with strong trust and he will help you. . . . When tempted, invoke your angel. He is more eager to help you than you are to be helped! Ignore the devil and do not be afraid of him; he trembles and flees at the sight of your guardian angel." One guardian angel, as God's spiritual bodyguard for each of us, is more powerful than all the demons of hell; so angels are good allies to have at our sides on our journey to heaven. Let us remember to pray to them each day for protection and guidance, for the more we get to know them and develop relationships with them, the more effective they can be in our lives.

COOL SAINT: ST. JOHN BOSCO

St. John Bosco, or "Don Bosco" as he is more popularly known, was no exception when it came to having a strong devotion to guardian angels. As an adult, Don Bosco turned the difficulties of his childhood—losing his father as a toddler, being raised by a single mother, having tensions and fights with his older brother and not enough money to afford an education—into an impetus to help young people in similar situations. He would go on to found the Salesian priests, brothers, and sisters to help young people in need through the gift of education and the challenge of holiness. All along Don Bosco's journey, his devotion to guardian angels helped him to fulfill this mission to young people, which God placed upon his heart at the age of nine.

Not everyone liked Don Bosco. Some people wanted to scare him into giving up his work with the young or even kill him. Many times during his life, Don Bosco's guardian angel would intervene in the form of a large gray dog that would appear out of nowhere in a moment of danger, fight off Don Bosco's attacker, and then vanish. At first Don Bosco thought this was just a simple dog, but time and time again it would appear at the right moment, no matter where he was, to protect him from those who would do him harm. One time Don Bosco managed to hold on to the dog and brought it back to the Oratory, the home he had created for the boys he had saved from the streets. Curious to see where this dog was from, Don Bosco put it in a locked room. When he went back to bring the dog food, the dog was gone, even though there had been no way for the animal to escape. Don Bosco knew then that the dog was a manifestation of his guardian angel, allowed by God to protect him in an extraordinary way. Since the dog was big and gray, Don Bosco dubbed the dog "Grigio," Italian for "gray."

St. John Bosco, pray for us.

FORGOTTEN PRAYER

O angel of God, my guardian dear, to whom God's love entrusts me here, ever this day be at my side, to light and guard, to rule and guide. Amen.

ACTIVITY

Some of the most beautiful art ever created has been religious art. Look online to find an image of the guardian angel that speaks to your heart. Print it out and keep it in a place where you will see it often. Decorate the area with a candle, flowers, or other symbolic items as a reminder to pray to your guardian angel. Let that space be an encouragement to frequently ask for the help of your guardian angel when faced with difficult situations or people. Angels are more than willing to help!

THIS IS NOT YOUR GRANDPARENTS' WAY OF EVANGELIZING

by Tommy Tighe

At our Baptism, we become missionaries of evangelization, and that calling only becomes further solidified at our Confirmation. And yet as Catholics we often feel awkward when we think about the mechanics of evangelization. We've compartmentalized it as a "Protestant thing" and seem to prefer to keep our faith to ourselves whenever we're out in the public square.

This reaction doesn't come from a place of shame but from a place of not really knowing what to do. So we go in search of the best means of evangelizing others and very quickly receive all kinds of feedback on how to move forward—everything from "Say 'Merry Christmas' instead of 'Happy Holidays'" to "Just smile and be joyful"—and yet it just doesn't seem to feel right.

And while all the apologists and Catholic media types mean well when they give their blueprint for spreading the Good News, I'm going to suggest that we would get a lot further on our mission of evangelization if we imitated a stand-up comedian.

I'll never forget when one of my wife's friends asked us if we had ever seen Jim Gaffigan's stand-up. We hadn't, but our curiosity was peaked when she mentioned that he was a Catholic with a big family. That very night, we jumped on Netflix and sat on the couch together watching *Mr. Universe*.

Since that time, we have been following Jim's career like total fangirls, enjoying every minute of his hilarious take on being the father of a bus-sized brood of kids. However, it was with the debut of *The Jim Gaffigan Show* on TV Land that I finally started to realize the value of his work. If you haven't seen the show, I would humbly suggest that you put this book down and head on over to the device of your choice to check it out (but don't forget to come back to the book and finish!).

For me, this show is a perfect road map for the New Evangelization. Jim and his wife, Jeannie (yes, she wrote the foreword to this book!), managed to put together a sitcom that appealed to the masses with its wide-reaching sense of humor while at the same time being unabashedly Catholic in a non-weird, non-proselytizing way. Pretty much all of the jokes were accessible to non-Catholics, and yet there were simple "Catholic clues" throughout the show that allowed all of us to feel as if we were a part of some great inside joke.

Their apartment has a crucifix and various Catholic statuary. The family attends Mass and are close friends with the parish priest; and let's face it, they have a ton of kids, and that's pretty much a Catholic-only thing at this point.

Somehow, the Gaffigans are able to toe the line of normal TV comedy and effective Catholic evangelization with perfection. People are finally able to see that we weirdo Catholics are actually pretty darn normal—and funny.

I'm not sure if Jim and Jeannie meant to do it, but the show piqued people's curiosity about the Catholic faith in a new and exciting way. The Gaffigans succeeded at creating something that is laugh-out-loud funny while at the same time opening the door for people to come home.

If you want to evangelize successfully, take a lesson from Jim Gaffigan's: eat some bacon, sit on your couch, and share the Good News.

COOL SAINT: ST. GENESIUS

St. Genesius of Rome was a comedian and an actor who performed in plays that routinely mocked Christianity. According to legend, during one of his plays that was mocking the sacrament of Baptism, Genesius had a profound conversion experience. He started to spread the Good News by means of his stage and refused to denounce Christianity despite being ordered to do so by Emperor Diocletian. And with that, he met the same fate as pretty much everyone else who refused to do what Diocletian asked.

Genesius is now considered as the patron saint of actors, clowns, comedians, dancers, musicians, and victims of torture.

St. Genesius, pray for us.

FORGOTTEN PRAYER

O my God, I love you above all things, with my whole heart and soul, because you are all good and worthy of all my love. I love my neighbor as myself for the love of you. I forgive all who have injured me, and I ask pardon of all whom I have injured. Amen.

ACTIVITY

Head on over to Netflix, and watch all of the Jim Gaffigan comedy specials they have available to you. He is laugh-out-loud funny without ever being crude, and he even manages to squeeze in some solid Catholic jokes in the process. After that, be sure to jump onto social media and follow both Jim and Jeannie. You're welcome.

YOUR UNUSUAL GIFTS

by Sr. Brittany Harrison

Most of us spent much our childhood trying to fit in and be cool. We invested time in learning skills that would gain us popularly and acclaim, mastering sports, video games, and the latest styles. We memorized song lyrics and information about famous people, and somehow, in the process, we discovered that we were good at some things and not at others. We developed gifts that brought us joy and a sense of fulfillment and experienced frustration at not being able to master every skill that we would like.

God has given each of us gifts that are tied to our missions and vocations in life. As we grow up, we have the exciting (and intimidating) task of uncovering our gifts and trying to discern what kind of lifestyle and profession we should adopt in order to be most fulfilled using these gifts. If we have a good spiritual foundation, we come to understand that our gifts are not given to us simply to help us gain popularity, fame, or fortune but also to serve others. As we read in Jesus' parable of the talents (see Matthew 25:14–30), we are entrusted with gifts to make them fruitful, not to hide them.

In 1 Corinthians 14:1, St. Paul encourages each of us: "Pursue love, but strive eagerly for the spiritual gifts." Among the spiritual gifts are those that Paul listed earlier in his letter to the Corinthians (see 1 Corinthians 12:7–11, 28–30; 13:1–3): wisdom, knowledge, faith, healing, prophecy, discernment of spirits, tongues, and interpretation of tongues. In Romans 12:6–8 he lists more gifts of the Spirit: faith, ministry, teaching, exhortation, giving, leadership, and mercy. These aren't the only gifts, either! God is generous, and even *more* gifts are listed in Isaiah 11:2–3. These are the ones most Catholics learn in Confirmation class—namely, the seven gifts of the Holy Spirit: wisdom, understanding, right judgment, knowledge, courage, reverence, and wonder and awe.

Why would God give ordinary people, like you and me, really awesome gifts such as being able to discern spirits and be gifted teachers? St. John Paul II explained: "The Holy Spirit, while bestowing diverse ministries in Church communion, enriches it still further with particular gifts or promptings of grace, called *charisms*. . . . The charisms are *received in gratitude* both on the part of the one who receives them, and also on the part of the entire Church. They are in fact a singularly rich source of grace for the vitality of the apostolate and for the holiness of the whole Body of Christ."[22]

Whatever gift we are entrusted with, whether it be a gift of hospitality or a gift of healing, is meant to lead us closer to Christ and to serve others. In fact, we don't even *own* the gifts given to us, because they are entrusted to us to make them fruitful, not handed over for us to do whatever we want with them. God will expect us to account for them at the end of our lives.

While some of the more "interesting" spiritual gifts, such as the ability to pray in tongues, might jump out at us when we read 1 Corinthians 12, St. Paul reminds us in 1 Corinthians 13 that while we might have tongues, prophecy, and incredible wisdom, if we don't have love for others, our gifts are nothing more than spiritual noise ("a resounding gong," no less!)—for "the greatest of these [gifts] is love" (1 Cor 13:13). Among all of the spiritual gifts we may set our hearts on, let us eagerly pray that love is the one gift that reigns over and sanctifies them all.

COOL SAINT:
BL. EUSEBIA PALOMINO

God often chooses those whom the world discards to be his strongest witnesses. Bl. Eusebia Palomino, by all outward appearances, was an insignificant child. She grew up in poverty, begging for food and fuel with her father, and never completed more than a cursory education. From the time of her First Communion, she felt the desire within her heart to give her life entirely to Jesus as a religious sister, but she did not know how her lack of education and poverty would make that possible.

Her first contact with the Salesian Sisters came when she began attending the Oratory school that the sisters had for young people in Salamanca, Spain. Quickly the sisters noted her gift with the younger children, who turned to her for counsel, wisdom, and encouragement in their difficulties. Drawing upon her gifts, the sisters soon gave her responsibilities in the Oratory. Her great desire was to become a Salesian Sister, which was eventually granted, after much struggle and uncertainty.

From first glance, many people assumed that Sr. Eusebia was just a petite, uneducated simpleton. She worked in the kitchen and answered the door. She had limited duties with the children, who enjoyed her storytelling. Although she seemed completely ordinary, the Holy Spirit looked upon her lowliness and enriched her with great spiritual gifts.

Sr. Eusebia was very devoted to the Eucharist and to our Lady, a hallmark of Salesian spirituality, and she strived to share that devotion with others, trying to get as many people as possible to consecrate themselves to Mary and to visit Jesus in the Blessed Sacrament. She also was entrusted with the gift of prophecy, predicting the Spanish Civil War and its persecution of the Catholic faith. She had a gift of healing and was able to help many people through her prayers. After the Spanish Civil War broke out, she asked God to accept her life as a sacrifice for peace to return to her country. She died on February 10, 1935, and was hailed a saint by many.

Bl. Eusebia Palomino, pray for us.

FORGOTTEN PRAYER

Oh Divine Jesus, alone in many tabernacles, without anyone to visit you and adore you, I offer you my solitary heart and desire that its every beat may be an act of love for you. Hidden in the Eucharist you never sleep, nor do you ever tire of going in search of sinners. Oh, loving Jesus! Oh solitary Gesù, how I wish that my heart could be a lamp whose light might radiate love for you alone . . . on guard for a sleeping world and for straying souls. . . . Amen!

—Bl. Eusebia Palomino

ACTIVITY

All of us are given spiritual gifts in order to enrich the Church, but many of us fail to recognize them. Looking at the list below, highlight the gifts you feel God may have entrusted to you. Some of them may surprise you! There are many more listed in scripture, but this list serves as a way to start to reflect on how God is acting in your life.

Mentioned in Isaiah 11:2–3 (Traditional Seven Gifts of the Holy Spirit):

- *Knowledge*—Knowledge helps us to know, in a convicted way, God's action in our lives. Knowledge is an intellectual comprehension of the faith.

- *Wisdom*—Wisdom allows us to share in God's perception of the world and situations. It helps us to properly order our life choices in relationship to our faith. This takes the gift of knowledge and roots it in our hearts.
- *Understanding*—Similar to wisdom, understanding leads us to grasp the essence of what God is trying to teach us in situations and experiences. It also grants us insight into the truths of the Catholic faith that go deeper than just mere words on a page. Understanding is strengthened through prayerful reflection.
- *Counsel*—Paired with prudence, counsel helps us to know what God is asking us to do in a situation. It also gives us the ability to guide others, through the help of the Holy Spirit.
- *Fortitude (Courage)*—Fortitude helps us to carry out what we understand through the gift of counsel. It gives us the ability to persevere in difficulties in order to remain faithful.
- *Piety*—Piety is prayerfulness and religious devotion, a desire to know and serve God out of love.
- *Fear of the Lord*—This gift is not fear as in terror but fear as in respect, motivated by love for God.

Mentioned in Romans 12:6–8:

- *Prophecy*—Prophesy is communicating to others an insight from the Holy Spirit either through word, action, or symbol.
- *Ministry*—Being called to a form of serving others is our ministry.
- *Teaching*—We are teaching when we share the faith or knowledge with others and are able to translate complex ideas into the language of the ones being taught.
- *Exhortation*—We support others through exhortation when we encourage others in what they are called to do in their lives and help them to persevere.
- *Generosity (Giving)*—Even if we do not have a lot of material things or money, we can still be generous. Some people have a special gift of generosity that goes beyond just giving stuff and also includes prayer, love, mercy, and so on.

- *Leadership*—God often chooses the weak and poor and makes them strong. Scripture is full of examples of the *anawim* (poor ones) whom God chooses as leaders (David, Mary, Peter, etc).
- *Acts of Mercy*—We are all called to perform the corporal and spiritual acts of mercy as an expression of our faith. Some people have a particular mission in relationship to this.

Mentioned in 1 Corinthians 12:8–30:

- *Faith*—Some people are gifted with a profound faith in God that moves mountains, as Jesus promised.
- *Healing*—When people with this gift pray for others, healing is experienced, which can be physical, spiritual, emotional, or a combination of all three. Whenever Jesus healed someone, he always healed the soul and emotional life in addition to the body.
- *Mighty Deeds*—Through the gift of faith, a person can sometimes be the channel through which God blesses others with incredible miracles.
- *Discernment of Spirits*—This gift, through prayer, enables a person to understand what is motivating a situation or person. This gift enables a person to be sensitive to the action of human or angelic spirits (good or bad).
- *Speaking in Tongues*—Since the time of the early Church, the Holy Spirit has gifted people with a special prayer language called "tongues." Sometimes this is even a human language not known to the person.
- *Interpretation of Tongues*—This is the ability to understand what a person with the gift of tongues is expressing in his or her prayer language.
- *Apostolic Service*—This can be related to those called to succeed the apostles in leadership of the Church—namely, the bishops.
- *Prophetic Living*—By our Baptism, all of us are called to be prophets and to witness by our lives to the truth of the Catholic faith. Often this demands that we be countercultural, which makes our living a prophetic statement.

- *Helping (Giving Assistance)*—Some people have a tremendous gift for knowing when others need help and generously assisting them. These people do so without a lot of fanfare and with great generosity.
- *Administration*—This refers to those entrusted with leading and guiding an organization or place.

CONCLUSION

Hipster culture is based on going against the trend, turning away from the mainstream; it's about the coolness of being a part of the ultimate counterculture.

All of these things could also be said about Catholicism. For two thousand years Catholics have been going against the trend, standing up in the face of the popular cultural beliefs of the day, and we've been epically cool, if I do say so myself. We've overcome every single culture that has come up against us, every single adversary who has tried to work on our demise.

Why?

Because the Catholic Church is not of this world. It is the living, breathing Body of Christ. If that wasn't the case, it would have died off years ago along with every other trend that has come and gone over time. Instead, the Catholic Church is the ultimate group of hipsters, the most counterculturally cool collection of individuals you have ever met.

We pray ancient prayers that haven't been said for millennia. We ask for the prayers of obscure and unknown saints who probably spend a great deal of time in heaven twiddling their thumbs, waiting for a request, and we interact in this culture and world through the lens of our traditional Catholic faith.

We like craft beer, farmers markets, and the latest trends in iPhone applications. We enjoy growing beards, wearing thick-rimmed glasses, and talking for hours about our favorite line from Flannery O'Connor.

At the same time, we kneel before the Blessed Sacrament in Eucharistic adoration; we chant along with the Latin being sung at the Extraordinary Form of the Mass; we invite priests to come over and hang out with our ridiculously large families; and we stand in awe of our Lord and the Church he has handed down to us.

We are Catholic hipsters. And while we may enjoy crunching on locally sourced kale chips and spinning vinyl records of music some have never heard of, whatever we do, we do it all for the glory of God.

ACKNOWLEDGMENTS

This book started out as a simple joke on Twitter—a simple joke about how silly it would be if a bunch of Catholics joined me in putting together a handbook of hipster Catholicism. The tweet got some mild recognition, if I'm being generous, but led to the one and only Lisa M. Hendey taking me seriously and referring me to Jonathan Ryan, an editor at Ave Maria Press, who told me to send him a pitch for the book!

To be honest, I thought it was insane to cold-e-mail someone who had never heard of me and pitch him a book based on a 140-character joke. But being new to writing for Lisa's Catholic Mom website, I agreed to follow her directions, mostly out of fear of being fired by my brand-new boss in the blogosphere.

What you hold in your hands is the result.

This book simply wouldn't exist without the fantastic work of a great cloud of contributors, and each and every one of them deserves a serious indulgence for working so hard to help pull this off. (I put in a request to Pope Francis but haven't heard back—I guess he's busy.)

Thank you Lisa Hendey, Sara Vabulas, Sr. Brittany Harrison, Melissa Keating, Fr. Kyle Schnippel, Mary Rezac, Anna Mitchell, Steven Lewis, Tiffany Walsh, Katherine Morna Towne, Arleen Spenceley, Leticia Ochoa Adams, Sergio Bermudez,

Matt Dunn, and Jeannie Gaffigan! Your contributions to the book are fun, creative, interesting, and authentically Catholic all at the same time. I am so proud to have worked with you on this book, and I look forward to sharing the profits from the eventual movie deal (I'm considering having Channing Tatum cast as me, but I'm open to other ideas).

Thank you, most of all, to my beautiful wife and children. It took Daddy a lot of time to put this book together, but the hard work paid off! Thank you for your support, for your love, and for being the light of my life even in the midst of darkness.

NOTES

1. "Augusto Czartoryski (1858–1893): Priest of the Salesians of Don Bosco," Vatican website, accessed March 27, 2017, http://www.vatican.va/news_services/liturgy/saints/ns_lit_doc_20040425_czartoryski_en.html.

2. "Buy a Pair, Give a Pair," *Warby Parker*, accessed March 27, 2017, https://www.warbyparker.com/buy-a-pair-give-a-pair.

3. Alban J. Dachaur, S.J. "Prayer of the Christian Farmer," in *Novena in Honor of St. Isidore: Patron of Farmers*, National Catholic Rural Life Conference. See https://www.catholicculture.org/culture/liturgicalyear/prayers/view.cfm?id=830.

4. If you want to learn more about Ignatian prayer, use the books of Fr. Timothy Gallagher, O.M.V. There is no substitute. This is coming from a girl who spent three years persuading broke college students to invest in the series while I attempted to teach them about prayer.

5. "Novena to Saint Benedict," *The Online Guide to Saint Benedict*, accessed March 30, 2017, http://www.e-benedictine.com/prayers.

6. Mariano Cera, quoted in Joseph Pronechen, "The Brown Scapular Still Sanctifies Souls," *National Catholic Register*, July 8, 2008, http://www.ncregister.com/site/article/the_brown_scapular_still_sanctifies_souls.

7. John Paul II, quoted in "Extracts from the address of His Holiness Pope John Paul II to the Plenary Meeting of the Congregation for Divine Worship and the Discipline of the Sacraments (21 September 2001)," *Catholic Culture*, accessed March 30, 2017, http://www.catholicculture.org/culture/library/view.cfm?recnum=4620#extracts.

8. Adapted from "The Brown Scapular," *Sisters of Carmel*, accessed June 4, 2017, http://www.sistersofcarmel.com/brown-scapular-information.php.

9. John Paul II, Papal Homily at the Mass with the Canonization of Twenty-seven New Saints, May 21, 2000, Vatican website, www.vatican.va.

10. "Ember Days," *New Advent*, accessed March 30, 2017, http://www. newadvent.org/cathen/05399b.htm.

11. This prayer is used by many in Catholic radio ministry. See, for example, https://saltandlightradio.com/prayer-requests.

12. Laura Wattenberg, quoted in Linda DiProperzio, "What Your Child's Name Says About You," *Parents*, accessed December 21, 2015. Full text available at http://www.parents.com/baby-names/ideas/getting-started/what-your-childs-name-says-about-you/#page=1.

13. Joal Ryan, *Puffy, Xena, Quentin, Uma: And 10,000 Other Names for Your New Millennium Baby* (New York: Plume, 1999).

14. St. John Paul II reminded us, "We are an Easter people and Alleluia is our song!" in his Angelus homily in Adelaide, Australia, November 30, 1986, Vatican website. Full text available at https://w2.vatican.va/content/john-paul-ii/en/angelus/1986/documents/hf_jp-ii_ang_19861130.html.

15. Peter Julian Eymund, "The Our Father, paraphrased by Saint Peter Julian Eymund," *CatholicSaints.Info*, accessed March 30, 2017, http://catholicsaints. info/the-our-father-paraphrased-by-saint-peter-julian-eymund.

16. Various ancient source texts vary between Jesus sending seventy or seventy-two disciples in pairs. Pope Benedict XVI, for instance, discusses this discrepancy in *Jesus of Nazareth: From the Baptism in the Jordan to the Transfiguration* (San Francisco: Ignatius Press, 2008), 179–180.

17. "A Morning Prayer Written by St. Thérèse," *EWTN*, accessed June 4, 2017, https://www.ewtn.com/Devotionals/prayers/therese3.htm.

18. Alban Butler, *Butler's Lives of the Saints: July*, ed. Peter Doyle (Collegeville, MN: Liturgical Press, 2000), 219.

19. "Dialogue Principles," *Dialogue Institute: Journal of Ecumenical Studies*, accessed June 4, 2017, http://dialogueinstitute.org/dialogue-principles.

20. "A Prayer before the Relics," *Cross Tipped Churches*, accessed June 4, 2017, http://crosstippedchurches.blogspot.com/2009/02/prayer-before-relics.html.

21. John Paul II, Homily at the Beatification of Pope John XXIII, September 3, 2000, Vatican website, www.vatican.va.

22. John Paul II, Apostolic Exhortation on the Vocation and the Mission of the Lay Faithful in the Church and in the World, December 30, 1988, §24, Vatican website, www.vatican.va.

ABOUT THE CONTRIBUTORS

Leticia Ochoa Adams is a regular on the Jennifer Fulwiler show on SiriusXM The Catholic Channel, a contributor at Aleteia, and a writer at *Through Broken Roses* on Patheos.

Sergio Bermudez is a Catholic writer who lives near Philadelphia, Pennsylvania. He enjoys people, places, and things.

Matt Dunn lives and works in suburban Philadelphia, where he is also a part-time professional musician and performs in a local concert band and as a member of an improvisational comedy troupe. Some of his religious poetry has been published at *The Great Adventure Blog* (biblestudyforcatholics.com/blog).

Sr. Brittany Harrison is a Salesian Sister of St. John Bosco and a high school campus minister. Her great passions in life include music, art, books, movies, technology, Grumpy Cat, and Jesus.

Lisa M. Hendey is the founder of, and advisor to *CatholicMom.com* and the author of *The Grace of Yes* and the *Chime Travelers* children's fiction series. Visit her at www.LisaHendey.com.

Melissa Keating is a writer and follicular hagiographer from St. Louis, Missouri. She attended Benedictine College before moving to Denver, Colorado, to serve as a FOCUS missionary and a journalist. She is now happily back in the land of great baseball and toasted ravioli, where she works for the Archdiocese of St. Louis. She is currently working on a novel and podcast, each of which have an estimated 30 percent chance of actually happening.

Steven Lewis is a California native with Bolivian blood and an allegedly Christian heart. As a FOCUS dropout, he conducts ministry for young adults and vlogs for Patheos at Patheos.com/blogs/SteveTheMissionary. His favorite Bible verse is Galatians 3:1, and you can find him on Twitter @SteveMissionary.

Anna Mitchell is the news director and producer of the *Son Rise Morning Show*, heard weekday mornings on the EWTN Global Catholic Radio Network. Check out the show online at www.SonRiseMorningShow.com.

Mary Rezac is a Nebraska-to-Colorado transplant and a staff writer at Catholic News Agency/EWTN News. The most hipster Catholic thing she has done is play her ukulele for Jesus during her breaks while teaching Totus Tuus, and she is not ashamed.

Fr. Kyle Schnippel was ordained for the Archdiocese of Cincinnati in 2004. He served as a high school teacher and Director of Vocations prior to becoming pastor of two parishes in northwest Cincinnati.

Arleen Spenceley is the author of *Chastity Is for Lovers: Single, Happy, and (Still) a Virgin*. She blogs at ArleenSpenceley.com.

Katherine Morna Towne blogs at *Sancta Nomina: Thoughts on Catholic Baby Naming* (sanctanomina.net), writes for *CatholicMom.com*, and has had several articles posted on *Nameberry*. You can find Kate as @SanctaNomina on Facebook, Twitter, and Instagram.

Sarah Vabulas's first book, *The Catholic Drinkie's Guide to Homebrewed Evangelism*, released in June 2015. She blogs at CatholicDrinkie.com.

Tiffany Walsh is a wife and mother to two precious children, a native Western New Yorker, and an academic librarian. She enjoys using humor in her writing, and she blogs about faith, books, and everything in between over at LifeofaCatholicLibrarian.com.

TOMMY TIGHE is a licensed marriage and family therapist who has worked in community mental health since 2006. He earned a bachelor's degree in psychology in 2003 from the University of California at Santa Barbara and a master's degree in clinical psychology from Antioch University in 2005.

Tighe has contributed to *Catholic Digest*, *Aleteia*, and *CatholicMom.com*. He records *The Catholic Hipster Podcast* with cohost Sarah Vabulas. He has appeared on Relevant Radio, EWTN Radio, and The Catholic Channel on SiriusXM Radio, which runs his podcast *The Chimney*.

He lives with his wife, Karen, in Livermore, California. They have four sons.

AVE
AVE MARIA PRESS

Founded in 1865, Ave Maria Press,
a ministry of the Congregation of
Holy Cross, is a Catholic publishing
company that serves the spiritual and
formative needs of the Church and its
schools, institutions, and ministers;
Christian individuals and families; and
others seeking spiritual nourishment.

For a complete listing of titles from

Ave Maria Press

Sorin Books

Forest of Peace

Christian Classics

visit www.avemariapress.com

AVE MARIA PRESS
Notre Dame, IN
A Ministry of the United States Province of Holy Cross